THE ULTIMATE SOURDOUGH DISCARD COOKBOOK

100 EASY AND NUTRITIOUS RECIPES FOR ECO-FRIENDLY AND HEALTH-CONSCIOUS BAKERS—YOUR ILLUSTRATED GUIDE TO SUSTAINABLE, ZERO WASTE HOME COOKING

ESME WHITMORE

TABLE OF CONTENTS

ABOUT THE AUTHOR

Meet Esme Whitmore, the creative mind and culinary innovator behind "The Ultimate Sourdough Discard Cookbook." With a passion for sustainable cooking and an unwavering dedication to the art of sourdough baking, Esme has transformed countless kitchens into havens of delicious and eco-friendly creations.

Esme's journey began in a cozy home kitchen, where her fascination with sourdough starter quickly blossomed into a lifelong pursuit of baking excellence. With years of experience as a professional baker and a background in nutrition, Esme combines scientific knowledge with an artistic flair, crafting recipes that are not only delectable but also health-conscious.

Esme's expertise is evident on every page of this cookbook. Each recipe reflects a deep understanding of the complexities and nuances of sourdough discard, turning what many consider waste into culinary treasures. From classic bread to innovative international delights, Esme's recipes are meticulously curated to inspire both novice bakers and seasoned chefs alike.

Beyond the kitchen, Esme is a passionate advocate for sustainable living. Through this cookbook, Esme aims to educate and empower others to reduce food waste while creating delicious meals that nourish the body and wow the taste buds. With a commitment to versatility and inclusivity, Esme ensures there are options for every dietary need and occasion.

Join Esme Whitmore on a transformative culinary journey with "The Ultimate Sourdough Discard Cookbook," and discover the endless possibilities of sourdough baking. Whether through detailed instructions, eco-friendly practices, or mouthwatering photos, Esme's expertise and passion shine through, making this cookbook an essential addition to any kitchen. Embrace the sourdough revolution and elevate your baking with Esme Whitmore's innovative and sustainable approach.

INTRODUCTION

For those new to the world of baking, sourdough is a treasured delight cherished for its complexity, flavor, and ancient heritage. Sourdough is naturally leavened bread made using a starter culture instead of commercial yeast.

The starter culture is a blend of wild yeast and beneficial bacteria that, when fermented, produce a tangy flavor and slightly chewy texture, adding complexity to the final product. Sourdough is primarily made with just flour, water, and salt. Fresh flour and water are necessary to maintain the culture's well-being. The process of creating sourdough requires creativity, patience, and dedication.

You can make sourdough with many types of flour, but you should start with the most readily available white bread flour. Good tap water is best for water, and fine pure sea salt is preferred, but if unavailable, any other cooking salt will do.

Sourdough baking is a time-honored tradition that enchants artisan bread enthusiasts and home bakers around the globe. In sourdough baking, sourdough discard is essential. The question now is: why is it so important?

Discard is an integral part of the sourdough process, helping to keep your sourdough starter active and manageable in quantity. Sourdough discard is the portion of the excess starter that is removed and set aside before feeding the remaining starter. This step is crucial to maintaining it active and healthy.

Maintaining the sourdough starter requires regular feeding. As a living ecosystem of microorganisms, the starter relies on fresh flour and water to receive essential nutrients. To preserve its sourness, right size, and hygiene, a good portion of the starter should be discarded regularly. Although sourdough is vital for making bread, the discard can be employed creatively in cooking and baking.

Finding creative uses for discard reduces waste and enables bakers to try different recipes and flavors, like pancakes, waffles, crackers, or even pizza crusts. The sourdough starter and discard are derived from the same ingredient but serve different functions and applications. But why has sourdough discard remained underappreciated for so long? The primary reasons lie in the modern baking industry's shift towards speed and convenience, overshadowing traditional slow and steady baking methods.

However, as we experience a resurgence in sourdough baking, there's an increasing trend of using every part of the starter, including the discard. Both home bakers and professional chefs are rediscovering the value of minimizing waste and maximizing flavors by incorporating discard into their culinary creations.

Apart from being a sustainable baking form, sourdough-baked products are superior to the usual loaf of bread made with commercial yeast. You may wonder if using the discarded portion of your sourdough starter provides the same fermentation benefits. Sourdough discard is a byproduct of maintaining your sourdough starter, but it is not trash. It has nutritional benefits similar to those of an active starter.

Here's why you shouldn't throw away your sourdough discard:

Promotes Gut Health: Like the active starter, sourdough discard contains lactic acid bacteria, beneficial probiotics that foster a healthy gut microbiome. These bacteria aid digestion, promoting overall digestive health.

Nutrient-rich: High in fiber, sourdough discard lowers cholesterol and helps control blood sugar levels. It also contains components that are essential for general health, including iron, magnesium, zinc, and B vitamins.

Enhances Flavor: Sourdough bread gets its distinctive tang from the lactic acid, formed during the fermentation process. Discarded dough can add this richness to baked products.

Improves Texture: Using discard can improve the texture of baked goods, adding slight chewiness or crispiness depending on the recipe.

You might be curious about different easy and delicious ways to use sourdough discard. For example, you can make pancakes and waffles by mixing your sourdough discard with flour, eggs, milk, and a sweetener of your choice to make them fluffy. A major mistake to avoid is substituting sourdough starter for liquid fat, as it can drastically change the texture of your baked products. Making sourdough crackers is another way to use sourdough discard; mix your discard with spices, herbs, and cheese to make crispy and flavorful crackers. This is an easy method as it allows you to collect large amounts of discard, spread it evenly on a sheet pan, and bake until crisp.

You may use sourdough discard to make a pizza crust, incorporating it into your pizza dough recipe. Other ways to use your discard include making biscuits and quick breads like banana bread. Sourdough discard would be useless if it didn't offer any advantages! Apart from containing essential vitamins, minerals, and fiber, sourdough discard fermentation often yields baked goods with a reduced glycemic index that aids in regulating blood sugar levels.

One common question is, "How do you add sourdough discard to a recipe?" This question will be answered in detail as you read through this book. However, the amount to use depends on the volume of discard. Feel free to use what you have, but for optimal results, add 113 to 227 grams of discard to a single dish, like a batch of cookies, unless you're working with minimal amounts.

The book you're about to read offers detailed knowledge of sourdough discard recipes you can try within your comfort zone. This book consists of healthy recipes made from nutritious ingredients, each created to help you achieve your wellness goals. Among the many options, there are Breakfast & Brunch recipes such as Pancakes and Muffins; Snacks & Appetizers like Crackers or Pretzel Bites; Lunch & Dinner options like Pizza Crust or Lasagna; Desserts such as Brownies or Cakes; and even Gluten-Free Options and International Delights! With step-by-step instructions, tips, and troubleshooting advice provided in this book, even beginners can confidently make delicious meals.

So, as you read, whether you are a professional chef, baker, or a newbie, let each chapter be more than just a read; let it be a call to action, inspiring you to try new things, experiment with new flavors, and push the boundaries beyond impossibilities. It's time to leap. With "The Ultimate Sourdough Discard Cookbook" in hand, you can never be stranded.

SOURDOUGH STARTER
RECIPES

CLASSIC SOURDOUGH STARTER

UTENSILS:
- Glass or ceramic container
- Measuring cups and spoons
- Kitchen scales
- Fork
- Silicone spatula

INGREDIENTS:
- 3/5 lb (1 cup) whole grain rye or whole wheat flour (preferably organic)
- 1.1 pounds (4 cups) all-purpose flour (preferably organic, excluding bleached flour)
- 1 quart (4 cups) filtered or spring water (room temperature)

INSTRUCTIONS:

Day 1: Making the Starter
- Record the weight of your jar before adding any ingredients. Mark the date you started preparing the starter on the jar with a marker.
- Combine 1/2 cup (3/5 lb or 100g) of flour with 1/2 cup (4 oz or 100g) of water in the jar. Mix thoroughly with a fork.
- Using a spatula, scrape down the edges of the dough.
- Cover the jar with a loose lid and leave it at room temperature for 24 hours.
- Mark the amount of starter in the jar with a marker to track its growth.

Day 2: No Changes
- There will probably be no visible change; leave it for another 24 hours.

Day 3: Visible Growth and Bubbles
- Set aside half of the starter (it is best to store the excess starter in the refrigerator in a sealed glass jar). There should be 1/2 cup (100g) of starter left in your jar.
- Add 1/2 cup (4 oz or 100g) of all-purpose flour and 1/2 cup (4 oz or 100g) of water. Stir well, scraping down the edges of the jar.
- Cover loosely again and let sit for 24 hours.

Day 4: More Bubbles
- Repeat the feeding process: discard half of the starter, leaving 1/2 cup (100g), and add 1/2 cup (4 oz or 100g) of fresh flour and 1/2 cup (4 oz or 100g) of water.
- Stir and scrape down the edges of the jar, then cover loosely.

Day 5: Continued Growth
- Discard and feed as before, keeping an eye out for growth and bubbles.

Days 6-7: Double Volume
- Repeat the feeding process.
- Stir, scrape, and cover. Continue this process until the starter doubles in size within 4-6 hours and begins to recede after 12 hours.
- Check if it peaks after 4-6 hours and has a pleasant sour smell. Test by dropping a tablespoon of starter into water; if it floats, it's ready!

Maintenance:
- **Frequent Bakers:** Store your starter at room temperature, discarding and feeding every 24 hours.
- **Occasional Bakers:** Store your starter in the refrigerator and feed it once a week. Allow the starter to sit at room temperature for 1-2 hours before refrigerating again.

WHOLE WHEAT SOURDOUGH STARTER

UTENSILS:

- Glass or ceramic container
- Measuring cups and spoons
- Kitchen scales
- Fork
- Silicone spatula

INGREDIENTS:

- 1.1 pounds (4 cups) whole wheat flour (preferably organic)
- 1 quart (4 cups) filtered or spring water (room temperature)

INSTRUCTIONS:

Day 1: Making the Starter
- Record the weight of your jar before adding any ingredients. Mark the date you started preparing the starter on the jar with a marker.
- Combine ½ cup of flour with ½ cup of water in the jar. Mix thoroughly with a fork.
- Using a spatula, scrape down the edges of the dough.
- Cover the jar with a loose lid and leave it at room temperature for 24 hours.
- Mark the amount of starter in the jar with a marker to track its growth.

Day 2: No Changes
- There will probably be no visible change; leave it for another 24 hours.

Day 3: Visible Growth and Bubbles
- Set aside half of the starter (it is best to store the excess starter in the refrigerator in a sealed glass jar). There should be ½ cup of starter left in your jar.
- Add ½ cup of whole wheatrye or whole wheatflour and ½ cup of water. Stir well, scraping down the edges of the jar.
- Cover loosely again and let sit for 24 hours.

Day 4: More Bubbles
- Repeat the feeding process: discard half of the starter, leaving ½ cup, and add ½ cup of fresh flour and ½ cup of water.
- Stir and scrape down the edges of the jar, then cover loosely.

Day 5: Continued Growth
- Discard and feed as before, keeping an eye out for growth and bubbles.

Days 6-7: Double Volume
- Repeat the feeding process.
- Stir, scrape, and cover. Continue this process until the starter doubles in size within 4-6 hours and begins to recede after 12 hours.
- Check if it peaks after 4-6 hours and has a pleasant sour smell. Test by dropping a tablespoon of starter into water; if it floats, it's ready!

Maintenance:
- **Frequent Bakers:** Store your starter at room temperature, discarding and feeding every 24 hours.
- **Occasional Bakers:** Store your starter in the refrigerator and feed it once a week. Allow the starter to sit at room temperature for 1-2 hours before refrigerating again.

GLUTEN-FREE SOURDOUGH STARTER (USING BROWN RICE FLOUR)

UTENSILS:

- Glass or ceramic container
- Measuring cups and spoons
- Kitchen scales
- Fork
- Silicone spatula

INGREDIENTS:

- 6 tablespoons (50g) brown rice flour
- ¼ cup (60ml) water
- 2 teaspoons freshly squeezed lemon juice

INSTRUCTIONS:

Day 1: Preparation
- Record the weight of your jar before adding any ingredients. Label the date you started making the starter on the jar with a marker.
- Mix 6 tablespoons (50g) of brown rice flour, ¼ cup (60ml) of water, and 2 teaspoons of lemon juice in the jar. Clean the edges of the jar.
- Place the jar in a warm place in the kitchen, and close the lid loosely.

Day 2: Initial Observations
- Stir the mixture and uncover it throughout the day. Smell the mixture; it should have a sweet smell.
- Keep the sides of the jar clean with a gentle spatula. Cover the jar loosely with a lid and keep it warm.

Day 3: Continue the Process
- Repeat the observations from the second day. Take out the starter, smell it, and stir.
- Scrape down the sides of the jar with a spatula to prevent mold. Keep covered and warm.

Day 4: Setting Up Consistency
- In the morning, smell the starter. Add ½ teaspoon (1.5g) of brown rice flour and stir.
- If the mixture is too thick, add a small amount of water. Stir, and cover with a lid. Stir again in the evening.

Day 5: Feeding and Observation
- Set aside half of the starter (it is best to store the excess starter in the refrigerator in a sealed glass jar) and add 6 tablespoons (50g) of brown rice flour and ¼ cup (60ml) of water in the morning.
- Let it rise or ferment with the lid closed. If it is too runny, add a teaspoon of brown rice flour.

Day 6: Sustained Growth
- In the morning, smell the starter. Remove a tablespoon of starter, add a tablespoon of brown rice flour, enough water, and stir.
- In the evening, add a tablespoon of flour and a little water. Stir, and cover with a lid. Check and stir again later, if desired.

Day 7: Final Preparations
- Check the readiness of the starter. Smell and listen to the bubbles burst with gentle stirring.
- This smaller portion creates about ¾ to 1 cup (approximately 200g), which is enough for some recipes.

Additional Tips:
- Consider transferring the starter to a larger bowl or glass jar if you need more than 200g for a recipe.
- Feed the starter on day 7 before bed so it is ready to bake on day 8.
- Save a spoonful of starter for the next batch.

Day 7: Continuation of the Cycle
- Take a large spoonful of starter and transfer it to a new jar before bed if you need to make a new batch of starter.
- Add a tablespoon of brown rice flour and enough water to cover. Leave it to ferment overnight.

Day 8: Starter is Ready
- When bubbles appear, stir the starter to activate it.
- Now you can add it to gluten-free recipes!

DRY STARTER REVIVAL

UTENSILS:

- Glass or ceramic container
- Measuring cups and spoons
- Kitchen scales
- Silicone spatula
- Fork

INGREDIENTS:

- 1 teaspoon (5g) dehydrated sourdough starter
- 1 tablespoon (15ml) water at 80°F
- 2 tablespoons (15g) all-purpose flour (preferably organic, excluding bleached flour)

INSTRUCTIONS:

Day 1: Preparing the Starter
- Record the weight of your jar before adding any ingredients. Label the date you started making the starter on the jar with a marker.
- In a jar, mix 1 teaspoon (5g) of dehydrated starter with 1 tablespoon (15ml) of water at room temperature.
- Leave the starter for about 2 hours.
- Stir in 2 tablespoons (15g) of flour.
- Mix thoroughly with a fork. Using a spatula, scrape down the edges of the dough.
- Cover the jar with a loose lid and leave it at room temperature for 12 hours.

Day 2: No Changes
- There will probably be no visible changes. Add another 1 tablespoon (10g) of flour and 2 teaspoons (10ml) of water.
- Mix thoroughly, scraping down the edges of the dough. Cover loosely with a lid.

Day 3: Visible Growth and Bubbles
- Add 1 tablespoon (10g) of flour and 2 teaspoons (10ml) of water.
- Stir well, scraping down the edges of the jar. Loosely close the lid again and leave for 24 hours at room temperature.

Day 4: More Bubbles
- Discard all the starter (it is best to store the excess starter in the refrigerator in a sealed glass jar), leaving only 1 tablespoon (15g).
- Add 2 tablespoons (30ml) of water and 2 tablespoons (30g) of flour.
- Stir, scrape down the edges of the jar, and cover loosely with the lid.

Day 5: Continued Growth
- In the morning, discard all the starter (it is best to store the excess starter in the refrigerator in a sealed glass jar), leaving only 1 tablespoon (15g).
- Add 2 tablespoons (30ml) of water and 2 tablespoons (30g) of flour.
- Stir, scrape down the edges of the jar, and cover loosely with the lid.
- In the evening, check the starter after about 7 hours. If it has almost tripled in size, repeat the same feeding as in the morning. If it hasn't peaked yet, wait another hour or two before checking again.

Day 6: Starter is Ready
- The starter should be completely ready for use.

BREAKFAST & BRUNCH

FLUFFY PANCAKES

Calories 180; Fat 6 g; Carb 27 g; Protein 5 g

SERVINGS: 12

PREP TIME: 10 minutes

COOKING TIME: 15-20 minutes

UTENSILS:

- Large mixing bowl
- Whisk
- Measuring cups and spoons
- Ladle or 1/4 cup measuring cup
- Non-stick skillet or griddle
- Spatula

INGREDIENTS:

- 1 cup (8 oz) sourdough discard
- 1 cup (4.5 oz) all-purpose flour
- 1 cup (8 fl oz) milk
- 1 large egg
- 2 tablespoons (1 oz) melted butter, plus more for cooking
- 1 tablespoon (0.5 oz) sugar
- 1 teaspoon baking powder
- 1/2 teaspoon baking soda
- 1/2 teaspoon salt
- 1 teaspoon vanilla extract

INSTRUCTIONS:

1. **Prepare the Wet Ingredients:**
- In a large mixing bowl, whisk together the sourdough discard, milk, egg, melted butter, and vanilla extract until well combined.
2. **Mix the Dry Ingredients:**
- In a separate bowl, whisk together the flour, sugar, baking powder, baking soda, and salt.
3. **Combine Wet and Dry Ingredients:**
- Gradually whisk in the dry ingredients until they are fully incorporated with the wet mixture. Do not overmix; some lumps are okay.
4. **Preheat the Skillet:**
- Heat a non-stick skillet or griddle over medium heat. Add a small amount of butter to the skillet to coat.
5. **Cooking the Pancakes:**
- Using a ladle or a 1/4 cup measuring cup, pour batter onto the skillet, forming pancakes. Cook until bubbles form on the surface of the pancakes and the edges look set, about 2-3 minutes.
6. **Flipping:**
- Carefully flip the pancakes and cook for an additional 1-2 minutes, until golden brown and cooked through.
7. **Repeat:**
- Repeat with the remaining batter, adding more butter to the skillet as needed.
8. **Serving:**
- Serve the pancakes warm with your favorite toppings such as maple syrup, fresh fruit, or whipped cream.
9. **Storage:**
- Store any leftover pancakes in an airtight container in the refrigerator for up to 2 days. Reheat in a toaster or microwave before serving.

WAFFLES

Calories 220; Fat 11 g; Carb 26 g; Protein 6 g

SERVINGS:

8

PREP TIME: 10 minutes   COOKING TIME: 20 minutes

UTENSILS:

- Large mixing bowl
- Whisk
- Measuring cups and spoons
- Waffle iron
- Ladle or 1/4 cup measuring cup
- Spatula

INGREDIENTS:

- 1 cup (8 oz) sourdough discard
- 1 1/2 cups (6.75 oz) all-purpose flour
- 1 cup (8 fl oz) milk
- 2 large eggs
- 1/4 cup (2 oz) melted butter, plus more for greasing the waffle iron
- 2 tablespoons (1 oz) sugar
- 1 teaspoon baking powder
- 1/2 teaspoon baking soda
- 1/2 teaspoon salt
- 1 teaspoon vanilla extract

INSTRUCTIONS:

1. **Prepare the Wet Ingredients:**
- In a large mixing bowl, whisk together the sourdough discard, milk, eggs, melted butter, and vanilla extract until well combined.
2. **Mix the Dry Ingredients:**
- In a separate bowl, whisk together the flour, sugar, baking powder, baking soda, and salt.
3. **Combine Wet and Dry Ingredients:**
- Gradually add the dry ingredients to the wet mixture, stirring until just combined. Be careful not to overmix; a few lumps are fine.
4. **Preheat the Waffle Iron:**
- Preheat your waffle iron according to the manufacturer's instructions. Lightly grease it with melted butter.
5. **Cooking the Waffles:**
- Using a ladle or a 1/4 cup measuring cup, pour batter onto the preheated waffle iron, spreading it out evenly. Close the waffle iron and cook until the waffles are golden brown and crisp, about 3-5 minutes, depending on your waffle iron.
6. **Removing the Waffles:**
- Carefully remove the waffles with a spatula and place them on a wire rack to keep them crisp while you cook the remaining batter.
7. **Repeat:**
- Repeat with the batter you have left.
8. **Serving:**
- Serve the waffles warm with your favorite toppings such as maple syrup, fresh fruit, or whipped cream.
9. **Storage:**
- Store any leftover waffles in an airtight container in the refrigerator for up to 2 days. Reheat in a toaster or oven before serving.

MUFFINS WITH BLUEBERRIES

Calories 180; Fat 6 g; Carb 29 g; Protein 4 g

SERVINGS:
12

PREP TIME: 15 minutes

COOKING TIME: 20-25 minutes

UTENSILS:

- Large mixing bowl
- Medium mixing bowl
- Whisk
- Measuring cups and spoons
- Muffin tin
- Paper muffin liners or non-stick cooking spray

INGREDIENTS:

- 1 cup (8 oz) sourdough discard
- 1 1/2 cups (6.75 oz) all-purpose flour
- 1/2 cup (4 oz) granulated sugar
- 1/2 cup (4 oz) milk
- 1/4 cup (2 oz) melted butter or vegetable oil
- 2 large eggs
- 1 teaspoon baking powder
- 1/2 teaspoon baking soda
- 1/2 teaspoon salt
- 1 teaspoon vanilla extract
- 1 cup (6 oz) add-ins such as blueberries, chocolate chips, or nuts (optional)

INSTRUCTIONS:

1. **Preheat the Oven:**
- Preheat your oven to 375°F (190°C). Line a muffin tin with paper liners or lightly grease with non-stick cooking spray.
2. **Prepare the Wet Ingredients:**
- In a large mixing bowl, whisk together the sourdough discard, milk, eggs, melted butter or vegetable oil, and vanilla extract until well combined.
3. **Mix the Dry Ingredients:**
- In a medium mixing bowl, whisk together the flour, sugar, baking powder, baking soda, and salt.
4. **Combine Wet and Dry Ingredients:**
- Gradually add the dry ingredients to the wet mixture, stirring until combined. Be careful not to overmix; some lumps are fine. If using add-ins like blueberries, chocolate chips, or nuts, gently fold them into the batter.
5. **Fill the Muffin Tin:**
- Using a spoon or a 1/4 cup measuring cup, evenly distribute the batter into the prepared muffin tin, filling each cup about 2/3 full.
6. **Baking:**
- Place the muffin tin in the preheated oven and bake for 20-25 minutes, or until the muffins are golden brown and a toothpick inserted into the center comes out clean.
7. **Cooling:**
- Allow the muffins to cool in the tin for about 5 minutes before transferring them to a wire rack to cool completely.
8. **Serving:**
- Serve the muffins warm or at room temperature. They can be enjoyed plain or with butter, jam, or honey.
9. **Storage:**
- Store any leftover muffins in an airtight container at room temperature for up to 3 days. They can also be frozen for longer storage. Reheat in the microwave or oven before serving.

SCONES

Calories 250; Fat 10 g; Carb 35 g; Protein 4 g

SERVINGS: 8

PREP TIME: 15 minutes   **COOKING TIME:** 20 minutes

UTENSILS:

- Large mixing bowl
- Medium mixing bowl
- Pastry cutter or forks
- Measuring cups and spoons
- Baking sheet
- Parchment paper

INGREDIENTS:

- 1 cup (8 oz) sourdough discard
- 2 cups (9 oz) all-purpose flour
- 1/4 cup (2 oz) granulated sugar
- 1 tablespoon baking powder
- 1/2 teaspoon salt
- 1/2 cup (4 oz) cold unsalted butter, cubed
- 1/2 cup (4 oz) heavy cream or milk
- 1 large egg
- 1 teaspoon vanilla extract
- 1 cup (6 oz) add-ins such as dried fruit, chocolate chips, or nuts (optional)
- Extra cream or milk for brushing the tops
- Coarse sugar for sprinkling (optional)

INSTRUCTIONS:

1. **Preheat the Oven:**
- Preheat your oven to 400°F (200°C). Line a baking sheet with parchment paper.
2. **Prepare the Dry Ingredients:**
- In a large mixing bowl, whisk together the flour, sugar, baking powder, and salt.
3. **Cut in the Butter:**
- Add the cold, cubed butter to the dry ingredients. Using a pastry cutter or forks, cut the butter into the flour mixture until it resembles coarse crumbs.
4. **Prepare the Wet Ingredients:**
- In a medium mixing bowl, whisk together the sourdough discard, heavy cream or milk, egg, and vanilla extract until well combined.
5. **Combine Wet and Dry Ingredients:**
- Gradually add the wet ingredients to the dry mixture, stirring until just combined. If using add-ins like dried fruit, chocolate chips, or nuts, gently fold them into the dough.
6. **Shape the Dough:**
- Turn the dough out onto a lightly floured surface and gently knead it a few times to bring it together. Pat the dough into a circle about 1 inch thick. Using a sharp knife, cut the circle into 8 wedges.
7. **Prepare for Baking:**
- Place the scones on the prepared baking sheet. Brush the tops with a bit of extra cream or milk and sprinkle with coarse sugar if desired.
8. **Baking:**
- Bake in the preheated oven for 15-20 minutes, or until the scones are golden brown and a toothpick inserted into the center comes out clean.
9. **Cooling:**
- Allow the scones to cool on the baking sheet for a few minutes before transferring them to a wire rack to cool completely.
10. **Serving:**
- Serve the scones warm or at room temperature. They can be enjoyed plain or with butter, jam, or clotted cream.
11. **Storage:**
- Store any leftover scones in an airtight container at room temperature for up to 2 days. They can also be frozen for longer storage. Reheat in the oven or microwave before serving.

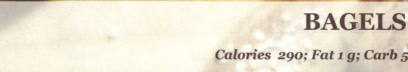

BAGELS

Calories 290; Fat 1 g; Carb 58 g; Protein 10 g

PREP TIME: 20 minutes   **RISING TIME:** 8-12 hours   **BAKING TIME:** 30-40 minutes

UTENSILS:

- Large mixing bowl
- Measuring cups and spoons
- Kitchen scale
- Baking sheet
- Parchment paper
- Large pot
- Slotted spoon
- Wire rack

INGREDIENTS:

- 1 cup (8 oz) sourdough discard
- 4 cups (17 oz) bread flour
- 1 1/2 cups (12 oz) warm water
- 1 tablespoon granulated sugar
- 2 teaspoons salt
- 1 tablespoon barley malt syrup or honey (for boiling water)
- Optional toppings: sesame seeds, poppy seeds, everything bagel seasoning, coarse salt, etc.

INSTRUCTIONS:

1. **Prepare the Dough:**
- In a large mixing bowl, combine the sourdough discard, bread flour, warm water, sugar, and salt. Mix until a rough dough forms.
2. **Kneading:**
- Turn the dough out onto a lightly floured surface and knead it for about 10 minutes until it becomes smooth and elastic. If the dough is too sticky, add a little more flour as needed.
3. **First Rise (Bulk Fermentation):**
- Place the dough back into the mixing bowl, cover it with a clean kitchen towel or plastic wrap, and let it rise at room temperature for 4-6 hours. Then transfer the dough to the refrigerator to ferment overnight (8-12 hours).
4. **Shaping:**
- The next morning, remove the dough from the refrigerator and let it come to room temperature. Divide the dough into 8 equal pieces. Shape each piece into a ball, then poke a hole through the center of each ball with your finger and gently stretch it to form a bagel shape. Place the shaped bagels on a baking sheet lined with parchment paper.
5. **Second Rise:**
- Cover the shaped bagels with a kitchen towel and let them rise at room temperature for about 1 hour, or until they have puffed up slightly.
6. **Preheat the Oven:**
- About 30 minutes before baking, preheat your oven to 425°F (220°C).
7. **Boiling:**
- Fill a large pot with water and bring it to a boil. Add the barley malt syrup or honey to the boiling water. Carefully add the bagels to the boiling water, a few at a time, and boil for 1-2 minutes on each side. Use a slotted spoon to remove the bagels from the water and place them back on the parchment-lined baking sheet.
8. **Adding Toppings:**
- If desired, sprinkle the tops of the bagels with your choice of toppings while they are still wet from boiling.
9. **Baking:**
- Place the baking sheet in the preheated oven and bake for 20-25 minutes, or until the bagels are golden brown.
10. **Cooling:**
- Remove the bagels from the oven and let them cool on a wire rack.
11. **Serving:**
- Serve the bagels fresh with your favorite spreads and toppings.
12. **Storage:**
- Store any leftover bagels in an airtight container at room temperature for up to 2 days. For longer storage, slice the bagels and freeze them. Reheat in a toaster or oven before serving.

QUICHE LORRAINE

Calories 330; Fat 22 g; Carb 25 g; Protein 5 g

SERVINGS:
6

PREP TIME: 30 minutes

COOKING TIME: 45-50 minutes

UTENSILS:

- Large mixing bowl
- Whisk
- Measuring cups and spoons
- Rolling pin
- Pie dish (9-inch)
- Aluminum foil or pie weights

INGREDIENTS:

Crust:
- 1 cup (8 oz) sourdough discard
- 1 1/2 cups (6.75 oz) all-purpose flour
- 1/2 cup (4 oz) cold unsalted butter, cubed
- 1/2 teaspoon salt
- 2-4 tablespoons cold water

Filling:
- 4 large eggs
- 1 cup (8 fl oz) heavy cream or half-and-half
- 1/2 teaspoon salt
- 1/4 teaspoon black pepper
- 1 cup (4 oz) shredded cheese (such as cheddar, Gruyère, or Swiss)
- 1/2 cup (2 oz) cooked bacon, ham, or sausage (optional)
- 1/2 cup (2 oz) chopped vegetables (such as spinach, mushrooms, or bell peppers, optional)
- 1/4 cup (1 oz) chopped onions or leeks (optional)

INSTRUCTIONS:

1. **Prepare the Crust:**
- In a large mixing bowl, combine the sourdough discard, flour, and salt. Add the cold, cubed butter and use a pastry cutter or forks to cut the butter into the flour mixture until it resembles coarse crumbs.
- Gradually add cold water, 1 tablespoon at a time, and mix until the dough comes together. Be careful not to overmix.
- Turn the dough out onto a lightly floured surface and shape it into a disk. Wrap it in plastic wrap and refrigerate for at least 30 minutes.
2. **Preheat the Oven:**
- Preheat your oven to 375°F (190°C).
3. **Roll Out the Dough:**
- On a lightly floured surface, roll out the chilled dough into a circle about 12 inches in diameter. Transfer it to a 9-inch pie dish, pressing it gently into the bottom and up the sides. Trim any excess dough hanging over the edges.
4. **Blind Bake the Crust:**
- Line the crust with aluminum foil or parchment paper and fill with pie weights or dried beans. Bake in the preheated oven for 15 minutes. Remove the foil and weights and bake for an additional 5 minutes, until the crust is lightly golden. Remove from the oven and set aside.
5. **Prepare the Filling:**
- In a large mixing bowl, whisk together the eggs, heavy cream or half-and-half, salt, and pepper. Stir in the shredded cheese, cooked meat, chopped vegetables, and onions or leeks, if using.
6. **Assemble the Quiche:**
- Pour the filling mixture into the pre-baked crust, spreading it out evenly.
7. **Bake the Quiche:**
- Bake in the preheated oven for 30-35 minutes, or until the filling is set and the top is golden brown. A knife inserted into the center should come out clean.
8. **Cooling:**
- Allow the quiche to cool for about 10 minutes before slicing and serving.
9. **Serving:**
- Serve the quiche warm or at room temperature. It can be enjoyed plain or with a side salad.
10. **Storage:**
- Store any leftover quiche in an airtight container in the refrigerator for up to 3 days. Reheat in the oven or microwave before serving.

FRENCH TOAST

Calories 190; Fat 8 g; Carb 24 g; Protein 6 g

SERVINGS: 4

PREP TIME: 10 minutes   **COOKING TIME:** 15-20 minutes

UTENSILS:

- Large mixing bowl
- Whisk
- Measuring cups and spoons
- Non-stick skillet or griddle
- Spatula
- Shallow dish

INGREDIENTS:

- 8 slices of day-old bread (preferably sourdough)
- 1 cup (8 oz) sourdough discard
- 1 cup (8 fl oz) milk
- 3 large eggs
- 2 tablespoons (1 oz) granulated sugar
- 1 teaspoon vanilla extract
- 1/2 teaspoon ground cinnamon (optional)
- 1/4 teaspoon salt
- Butter or oil for cooking
- Toppings: maple syrup, powdered sugar, fresh fruit, or whipped cream

INSTRUCTIONS:

1. **Prepare the Batter:**
- In a large mixing bowl, whisk together the sourdough discard, milk, eggs, sugar, vanilla extract, ground cinnamon (if using), and salt until well combined.
2. **Soak the Bread:**
- Pour the batter into a shallow dish. Dip each slice of bread into the batter, ensuring both sides are well coated. Allow the bread to soak for about 1-2 minutes on each side to absorb the batter.
3. **Preheat the Skillet:**
- Heat a non-stick skillet or griddle over medium heat. Add a small amount of butter or oil to coat the surface.
4. **Cooking the French Toast:**
- Place the soaked bread slices onto the preheated skillet. Cook until golden brown, about 3-4 minutes on each side. Flip the slices with a spatula and cook the other side until golden brown and cooked through.
5. **Repeat:**
- Repeat the process with the remaining slices of bread, adding more butter or oil to the skillet as needed.
6. **Serving:**
- Serve the French toast warm with your favorite toppings such as maple syrup, powdered sugar, fresh fruit, or whipped cream.
7. **Storage:**
- Store any leftover French toast in an airtight container in the refrigerator for up to 2 days. Reheat in the toaster or oven before serving.

CINNAMON ROLLS

Calories 320; Fat 12 g; Carb 47 g; Protein 5 g

SERVINGS:
12

PREP TIME: 20 minutes | RISING TIME: 8-12 hours | BAKING TIME: 25-30 minutes

UTENSILS:

- Large mixing bowl
- Measuring cups and spoons
- Rolling pin
- Dough scraper or knife
- Baking dish (9x13 inch)
- Small mixing bowl
- Whisk

INGREDIENTS:

Dough:
- 1 cup (8 oz) sourdough discard
- 3 cups (13.5 oz) all-purpose flour
- 1/2 cup (4 oz) warm milk
- 1/4 cup (2 oz) granulated sugar
- 1/4 cup (2 oz) unsalted butter, melted
- 1 large egg
- 1 teaspoon salt
- 1 teaspoon vanilla extract
- 1 teaspoon instant yeast (optional, for a quicker rise)

Filling:
- 1/2 cup (4 oz) unsalted butter, softened
- 1 cup (7.5 oz) brown sugar
- 2 tablespoons ground cinnamon

Icing:
- 1 cup (4 oz) powdered sugar
- 2 tablespoons (1 oz) milk
- 1 teaspoon vanilla extract

INSTRUCTIONS:

1. **Prepare the Dough:**
- In a large mixing bowl, combine the sourdough discard, flour, warm milk, sugar, melted butter, egg, salt, vanilla extract, and instant yeast (if using). Mix until a rough dough forms.
2. **Kneading:**
- Turn the dough out onto a lightly floured surface and knead for about 10 minutes until it becomes smooth and elastic. If the dough is too sticky, add a little more flour as needed.
3. **First Rise (Bulk Fermentation):**
- Place the dough back into the mixing bowl, cover it with a clean kitchen towel or plastic wrap, and let it rise at room temperature for 4-6 hours. Then transfer the dough to the refrigerator to ferment overnight (8-12 hours).
4. **Shaping:**
- The next morning, remove the dough from the refrigerator and let it come to room temperature. Roll the dough out on a lightly floured surface into a rectangle about 12x18 inches.
5. **Prepare the Filling:**
- In a small mixing bowl, combine the softened butter, brown sugar, and cinnamon. Spread the mixture evenly over the rolled-out dough.
6. **Rolling and Cutting:**
- Starting from one of the long edges, tightly roll the dough into a log. Use a dough scraper or knife to cut the log into 12 even slices.
7. **Second Rise:**
- Place the slices into a greased 9x13 inch baking dish. Cover with a kitchen towel and let them rise at room temperature for 1-2 hours, or until they have puffed up and are touching each other.
8. **Preheat the Oven:**
- About 30 minutes before baking, preheat your oven to 350°F (175°C).
9. **Baking:**
- Bake the cinnamon rolls in the preheated oven for 25-30 minutes, or until they are golden brown and cooked through.
10. **Prepare the Icing:**
- While the cinnamon rolls are baking, whisk together the powdered sugar, milk, and vanilla extract in a small mixing bowl until smooth.
11. **Icing the Rolls:**
- Remove the cinnamon rolls from the oven and let them cool for about 10 minutes. Drizzle the icing over the warm rolls.
12. **Serving:**
- Serve the cinnamon rolls warm.
13. **Storage:**
- Store any leftover cinnamon rolls in an airtight container at room temperature for up to 2 days. Reheat in the microwave or oven before serving.

FRENCH CREPES

Calories 110; Fat 4 g; Carb 13 g; Protein 4 g

SERVINGS:

12

PREP TIME: 10 minutes	RISING TIME: 30 minutes	BAKING TIME: 20 minutes

UTENSILS:

- Large mixing bowl
- Whisk
- Measuring cups and spoons
- Blender (optional)
- Non-stick skillet or crepe pan
- Spatula
- Ladle or 1/4 cup measuring cup

INGREDIENTS:

- 1 cup (8 oz) sourdough discard
- 1 cup (8 oz) all-purpose flour
- 1 1/2 cups (12 oz) milk
- 3 large eggs
- 2 tablespoons (1 oz) melted butter, plus more for cooking
- 1 tablespoon granulated sugar (optional, for sweet crepes)
- 1 teaspoon vanilla extract (optional, for sweet crepes)
- 1/4 teaspoon salt

INSTRUCTIONS:

1. **Prepare the Batter:**
- In a large mixing bowl, whisk together the sourdough discard, flour, milk, eggs, melted butter, sugar (if using), vanilla extract (if using), and salt until smooth. Alternatively, you can blend the ingredients in a blender until smooth.
- Let the batter rest for at least 30 minutes to allow the flour to hydrate and the bubbles to dissipate.
2. **Preheat the Skillet:**
- Heat a non-stick skillet or crepe pan over medium heat. Lightly grease the skillet with a small amount of butter.
3. **Cooking the Crepes:**
- Pour a small amount of batter (about 1/4 cup) into the center of the skillet. Immediately tilt and rotate the skillet to spread the batter evenly into a thin layer.
- Cook the crepe for about 1-2 minutes, or until the edges start to lift and the underside is lightly golden. Use a spatula to flip the crepe and cook for an additional 1-2 minutes on the other side.
4. **Repeat:**
- Transfer the cooked crepe to a plate and cover with a clean kitchen towel to keep warm. Repeat with the remaining batter, adding more butter to the skillet as needed.
5. **Serving:**
- Serve the crepes warm with your favorite fillings and toppings. For sweet crepes, try fillings like Nutella, fresh fruit, whipped cream, or powdered sugar. For savory crepes, try fillings like ham, cheese, sautéed vegetables, or scrambled eggs.
6. **Storage:**
- Store any leftover crepes in an airtight container in the refrigerator for up to 2 days. Reheat in the microwave or skillet before serving.

BREAKFAST BISCUITS

Calories 210; Fat 10 g; Carb 25 g; Protein 4 g

SERVINGS:
12

PREP TIME: 15 minutes   COOKING TIME: 15-18 minutes

UTENSILS:

- Large mixing bowl
- Measuring cups and spoons
- Pastry cutter or forks
- Baking sheet
- Parchment paper or silicone baking mat
- Rolling pin (optional)
- Biscuit cutter or round cookie cutter

INGREDIENTS:

- 1 cup (8 oz) sourdough discard
- 2 cups (9 oz) all-purpose flour
- 1 tablespoon baking powder
- 1/2 teaspoon baking soda
- 1 teaspoon salt
- 1 tablespoon granulated sugar
- 1/2 cup (4 oz) cold unsalted butter, cubed
- 3/4 cup (6 oz) buttermilk (or regular milk with 1 tablespoon vinegar or lemon juice)

INSTRUCTIONS:

1. **Preheat the Oven:**
- Preheat your oven to 425°F (220°C). Line a baking sheet with parchment or a silicone baking mat.
2. **Prepare the Dry Ingredients:**
- In a large mixing bowl, whisk together the flour, baking powder, baking soda, salt, and sugar.
3. **Cut in the Butter:**
- Add the cold, cubed butter to the dry ingredients. Use a pastry cutter or forks to cut the butter into the flour mixture until it resembles coarse crumbs.
4. **Combine Wet Ingredients:**
- In a separate bowl, mix the sourdough discard and buttermilk until well combined.
5. **Form the Dough:**
- Gradually add the wet mixture to the dry ingredients, stirring until just combined. Be careful not to overmix; the dough should be slightly sticky and shaggy.
6. **Shaping the Biscuits:**
- Turn the dough out onto a lightly floured surface. Gently pat the dough into a rectangle about 1 inch thick. If desired, use a rolling pin to ensure even thickness.
- Use a biscuit cutter or round cookie cutter to cut out biscuits. Place the biscuits on the prepared baking sheet. Gather any scraps, gently press together, and cut out more biscuits.
7. **Baking:**
- Bake the biscuits in the preheated oven for 15-18 minutes, or until they are golden brown on top.
8. **Cooling:**
- Allow the biscuits to cool on a wire rack for a few minutes before serving.
9. **Serving:**
- Serve the biscuits warm with butter, jam, honey, or as part of a breakfast sandwich with eggs, bacon, or sausage.
10. **Storage:**
- Store any leftover biscuits in an airtight container at room temperature for up to 2 days. Reheat in the oven or microwave before serving.

BREADS & ROLLS

ARTISAN BREAD

Calories 140; Fat 1 g; Carb 28 g; Protein 5 g

PREP TIME: 20 minutes	RISING TIME: 8-12 hours	BAKING TIME: 30-35 minutes

UTENSILS:

- Large mixing bowl
- Measuring cups and spoons
- Kitchen scale
- Dutch oven or baking stone
- Parchment paper
- Sharp knife
- Clean kitchen towel or plastic wrap

INGREDIENTS:

- 1 cup (8 oz) sourdough discard
- 4 cups (17 oz) bread flour
- 1 1/2 cups (12 oz) warm water
- 2 teaspoons salt
- 1 teaspoon instant yeast (optional, for a quicker rise)

INSTRUCTIONS:

1. **Prepare the Dough:**
- In a large mixing bowl, combine the sourdough discard, bread flour, warm water, salt, and instant yeast (if using). Mix until a rough dough forms.
2. **Kneading:**
- Turn the dough out onto a lightly floured surface and knead it for about 10 minutes until it becomes smooth and elastic. If the dough is too sticky, add a little more flour as needed.
3. **First Rise (Bulk Fermentation):**
- Place the dough back into the mixing bowl, cover it with a clean kitchen towel or plastic wrap, and let it rise at room temperature for 4-6 hours. Then transfer the dough to the refrigerator to ferment overnight (8-12 hours).
4. **Shaping:**
- The next morning, remove the dough from the refrigerator and let it come to room temperature. Turn the dough out onto a lightly floured surface and gently shape it into a round or oval loaf.
5. **Second Rise:**
- Place the shaped dough on a piece of parchment paper. Cover it with a clean kitchen towel and let it rise at room temperature for 2-3 hours, or until it has doubled in size.
6. **Preheat the Oven:**
- About 30 minutes before baking, preheat your oven to 450°F (230°C). If using a Dutch oven, place it in the oven to preheat.
7. **Scoring:**
- Once the dough has finished its second rise, use a sharp knife or lame to make a few slashes on the top of the loaf. This allows the bread to expand while baking.
8. **Baking:**
- If using a Dutch oven, carefully remove it from the oven and place the dough (with the parchment paper) inside. Cover with the lid and bake for 20 minutes. Remove the lid and bake for an additional 10-15 minutes, or until the bread is golden brown and sounds hollow when tapped on the bottom.
- If using a baking stone, slide the parchment paper with the dough onto the preheated stone. Bake for 30-35 minutes, or until the bread is golden brown and sounds hollow when tapped on the bottom.
9. **Cooling:**
- Remove the bread from the oven and let it cool on a wire rack for at least 1 hour before slicing.
10. **Serving:**
- Serve the artisan bread sliced, with butter, olive oil, or your favorite toppings.
11. **Storage:**
- Store any leftover bread in an airtight container at room temperature for up to 2 days. For longer storage, slice and freeze the bread, then reheat in the oven or toaster before serving.

BAGUETTES

Calories 80; Fat 1 g; Carb 16 g; Protein 3 g

SERVINGS: 3

PREP TIME: 30 minutes **RISING TIME:** 8-12 hours **BAKING TIME:** 25-30 minutes

UTENSILS:

- Large mixing bowl
- Measuring cups and spoons
- Kitchen scale
- Clean kitchen towel or plastic wrap
- Baking sheet or baguette pan
- Parchment paper
- Sharp knife
- Clean kitchen towel

INGREDIENTS:

- 1 cup (8 oz) sourdough discard
- 4 cups (17 oz) bread flour
- 1 1/2 cups (12 oz) warm water
- 2 teaspoons salt
- 1 teaspoon instant yeast (optional, for a quicker rise)

INSTRUCTIONS:

1. **Prepare the Dough:**
- In a large mixing bowl, combine the sourdough discard, bread flour, warm water, salt, and instant yeast (if using). Mix until a rough dough forms.
2. **Kneading:**
- Turn the dough out onto a lightly floured surface and knead it for about 10 minutes until it becomes smooth and elastic. If the dough is too sticky, add a little more flour as needed.
3. **First Rise (Bulk Fermentation):**
- Place the dough back into the mixing bowl, cover it with a clean kitchen towel or plastic wrap, and let it rise at room temperature for 4-6 hours. Then transfer the dough to the refrigerator to ferment overnight (8-12 hours).
4. **Shaping:**
- The next morning, remove the dough from the refrigerator and let it come to room temperature. Divide the dough into three equal pieces. Shape each piece into a rough rectangle. Fold the long sides of each rectangle toward the center, then roll the dough into a log, tapering the ends slightly to form the baguette shape.
5. **Second Rise:**
- Place the shaped baguettes on a parchment-lined baking sheet or baguette pan. Cover with a clean kitchen towel and let them rise at room temperature for 2-3 hours, or until they have doubled in size.
6. **Preheat the Oven:**
- About 30 minutes before baking, preheat your oven to 475°F (245°C). Place a shallow pan of water on the bottom rack of the oven to create steam, which helps develop a crisp crust.
7. **Scoring:**
- Once the baguettes have finished their second rise, use a sharp knife or lame to make several diagonal slashes on the top of each loaf. This allows the bread to expand while baking.
8. **Baking:**
- Place the baguettes in the preheated oven. Bake for 25-30 minutes, or until the baguettes are golden brown and sound hollow when tapped on the bottom.
9. **Cooling:**
- Remove the baguettes from the oven and let them cool on a wire rack for at least 30 minutes before slicing.
10. **Serving:**
- Serve the baguettes warm or at room temperature. They can be enjoyed plain, with butter, or used for sandwiches.
11. **Storage:**
- Store any leftover baguettes in an airtight container at room temperature for up to 2 days. For longer storage, freeze the baguettes, then reheat in the oven before serving.

SANDWICH LOAVES

Calories 70; Fat 1 g; Carb 14 g; Protein 2 g

SERVINGS:

2

PREP TIME: 20 minutes	RISING TIME: 8-12 hours	BAKING TIME: 35-40 minutes

UTENSILS:

- Large mixing bowl
- Measuring cups and spoons
- Kitchen scale
- Clean kitchen towel or plastic wrap
- Two 9x5 inch loaf pans
- Parchment paper (optional)
- Sharp knife

INGREDIENTS:

- 1 cup (8 oz) sourdough discard
- 6 cups (25.5 oz) bread flour
- 2 cups (16 oz) warm water
- 2 tablespoons granulated sugar
- 2 teaspoons salt
- 2 tablespoons unsalted butter, melted
- 2 teaspoons instant yeast (optional, for a quicker rise)

INSTRUCTIONS:

1. **Prepare the Dough:**
- In a large mixing bowl, combine the sourdough discard, bread flour, warm water, sugar, salt, melted butter, and instant yeast (if using). Mix until a rough dough forms.
2. **Kneading:**
- Turn the dough out onto a lightly floured surface and knead for about 10 minutes until it becomes smooth and elastic. If the dough is too sticky, add a little more flour as needed.
3. **First Rise (Bulk Fermentation):**
- Place the dough back into the mixing bowl, cover it with a clean kitchen towel or plastic wrap, and let it rise at room temperature for 4-6 hours. Then transfer the dough to the refrigerator to ferment overnight (8-12 hours).
4. **Shaping:**
- The next morning, remove the dough from the refrigerator and let it come to room temperature. Divide the dough into two equal pieces. Shape each piece into a rectangle, then roll tightly from the short side to form a log. Pinch the seam and ends to seal.
5. **Second Rise:**
- Grease two 9x5 inch loaf pans or line them with parchment paper. Place each shaped log into the prepared loaf pans. Cover with a clean kitchen towel and let them rise at room temperature for 2-3 hours, or until the dough has risen to about 1 inch above the rim of the pans.
6. **Preheat the Oven:**
- About 30 minutes before baking, preheat your oven to 375°F (190°C).
7. **Baking:**
- Place the loaf pans in the preheated oven and bake for 35-40 minutes, or until the loaves are golden brown and sound hollow when tapped on the bottom. If the tops are browning too quickly, cover loosely with aluminum foil.
8. **Cooling:**
- Remove the loaves from the oven and let them cool in the pans for 10 minutes. Then transfer the loaves to a wire rack to cool completely before slicing.
9. **Serving:**
- Slice the sandwich loaves and serve as desired. They are perfect for sandwiches, toast, or simply with butter and jam.
10. **Storage:**
- Store any leftover bread in an airtight container at room temperature for up to 3 days. For longer storage, slice and freeze the bread, then reheat in the toaster or oven before serving.

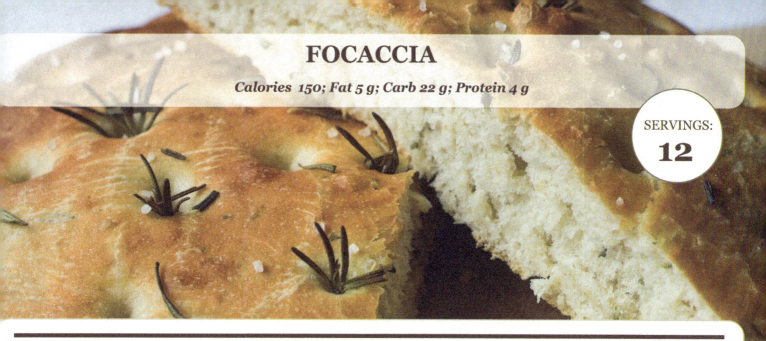

FOCACCIA

Calories 150; Fat 5 g; Carb 22 g; Protein 4 g

SERVINGS:
12

PREP TIME: 15 minutes	RISING TIME: 5-8 hours	BAKING TIME: 22-25 minutes

UTENSILS:

- Large mixing bowl
- Measuring cups and spoons
- Kitchen scale
- Sheet pan
- Parchment paper

INGREDIENTS:

- 2 cups (8 oz) bread flour
- 1 1/2 cups (6 oz) sourdough discard
- 3/4 cup (6 oz) warm water
- 1 teaspoon salt
- 2 tablespoons (about 2 fl oz) olive oil, plus more for drizzling
- 1 teaspoon dried herbs (such as rosemary, thyme, or oregano)
- Coarse sea salt, for sprinkling

INSTRUCTIONS:

1. **Prepare the Sourdough Starter:**
- Ensure your sourdough discard is active and bubbly before using it in the recipe. If it has been stored in the refrigerator, take it out and let it come to room temperature.
2. **Mixing the Dough:**
- In a large mixing bowl, combine the bread flour, sourdough discard, warm water, and salt. Mix until all the ingredients are fully incorporated and a dough forms.
3. **Kneading:**
- Turn the dough out onto a lightly floured surface and knead it for about 5-7 minutes until it becomes smooth and elastic.
4. **First Rise (Bulk Fermentation):**
- Place the dough back into the mixing bowl, cover it with a clean kitchen towel, and let it ferment at room temperature for about 4-6 hours, or until it has doubled in size.
5. **Shaping:**
- Once the dough has doubled in size, gently deflate it and transfer it to a baking sheet lined with parchment paper. Using your hands, gently press and stretch the dough to fill the baking sheet evenly.
6. **Second Rise:**
- Cover the shaped dough with a kitchen towel and let it rise for another 1-2 hours, or until it has increased in size by about 50%.
7. **Preheat the Oven:**
- About 30 minutes before baking, preheat your oven to 425°F (220°C).
8. **Adding Toppings:**
- Using your fingertips, make dimples all over the surface of the dough. Drizzle olive oil generously over the dough, allowing it to pool in the dimples. Sprinkle dried herbs and coarse sea salt evenly over the top.
9. **Baking:**
- Place the baking sheet in the preheated oven and bake for 20-25 minutes, or until the focaccia is golden brown on top and sounds hollow when tapped on the bottom.
10. **Cooling:**
- Once baked, remove the focaccia from the oven and let it cool on a wire rack for at least 10 minutes before slicing and serving.
11. **Serving:**
- Focaccia is best enjoyed warm. You can serve it plain, as an accompaniment to soups or salads, or slice it horizontally to make sandwiches. It also pairs wonderfully with a side of olive oil and balsamic vinegar for dipping.
12. **Storage:**
- Store any leftover focaccia in an airtight container at room temperature for up to 2 days. It's best enjoyed fresh, but you can also freeze leftover slices for longer storage.

PRETZEL ROLLS

Calories 180; Fat 3 g; Carb 34 g; Protein 5 g

SERVINGS:
8

| PREP TIME: 30 minutes | RISING TIME: 1-2 hours | BAKING TIME: 15-20 minutes |

UTENSILS:

- Large mixing bowl
- Measuring cups and spoons
- Kitchen scale
- Clean kitchen towel or plastic wrap
- Baking sheet
- Parchment paper or silicone baking mat
- Large pot
- Slotted spoon
- Sharp knife or lame

INGREDIENTS:

- 1 cup (8 oz) sourdough discard
- 3 cups (13.5 oz) bread flour
- 1 cup (8 oz) warm water
- 2 tablespoons unsalted butter, melted
- 1 tablespoon granulated sugar
- 2 teaspoons salt
- 1 teaspoon instant yeast (optional, for a quicker rise)

For the boiling solution:
- 10 cups water
- 1/2 cup baking soda

Topping:
- Coarse sea salt, for sprinkling

INSTRUCTIONS:

1. **Prepare the Dough:**
- In a large mixing bowl, combine the sourdough discard, bread flour, warm water, melted butter, sugar, salt, and instant yeast (if using). Mix until a rough dough forms.
2. **Kneading:**
- Turn the dough out onto a lightly floured surface and knead for about 10 minutes until it becomes smooth and elastic. If the dough is too sticky, add a little more flour as needed.
3. **First Rise:**
- Place the dough back into the mixing bowl, cover it with a clean kitchen towel or plastic wrap, and let it rise at room temperature for 1-2 hours, or until it has doubled in size.
4. **Shaping:**
- Once the dough has risen, turn it out onto a lightly floured surface and divide it into 8 equal pieces. Shape each piece into a ball by pulling the edges under and pinching them together at the bottom to create a smooth top.
5. **Second Rise:**
- Place the shaped rolls on a baking sheet lined with parchment paper or a silicone baking mat. Cover with a clean kitchen towel and let them rise for another 30-45 minutes, or until they have puffed up slightly.
6. **Preheat the Oven:**
- About 30 minutes before baking, preheat your oven to 425°F (220°C).
7. **Prepare the Boiling Solution:**
- In a large pot, bring 10 cups of water to a boil. Carefully add the baking soda to the boiling water.
8. **Boiling:**
- Using a slotted spoon, carefully lower each roll into the boiling water, one or two at a time. Boil for 30 seconds on each side, then remove with the slotted spoon and return to the baking sheet. Repeat with the remaining rolls.
9. **Scoring and Topping:**
- Use a sharp knife or lame to make a shallow X-shaped slash on the top of each roll. Sprinkle the tops with coarse sea salt.
10. **Baking:**
- Place the baking sheet in the preheated oven and bake for 15-20 minutes, or until the pretzel rolls are deep golden brown and sound hollow when tapped on the bottom.
11. **Cooling:**
- Remove the pretzel rolls from the oven and let them cool on a wire rack for at least 10 minutes before serving.
12. **Serving:**
- Serve the pretzel rolls warm or at room temperature. They can be enjoyed plain, with butter, or used for sandwiches.
13. **Storage:**
- Store any leftover pretzel rolls in an airtight container at room temperature for up to 2 days. For longer storage, freeze the rolls and reheat in the oven before serving.

"GOLDEN" ROLLS

Calories 90; Fat 2 g; Carb 15 g; Protein 3 g

SERVINGS:
12

PREP TIME: 20 minutes   **RISING TIME:** 4-6 hours   **BAKING TIME:** 20-25 minutes

UTENSILS:

- Large mixing bowl
- Measuring cups and spoons
- Kitchen scale
- Sheet pan
- Parchment paper

INGREDIENTS:

- 1 cup (8 oz) sourdough discard
- 3 cups (13.5 oz) all-purpose flour
- 3/4 cup (6 oz) warm water
- 1/4 cup (2 oz) unsalted butter, melted
- 2 tablespoons granulated sugar
- 1 1/2 teaspoons salt
- 1 teaspoon instant yeast (optional, for a quicker rise)

INSTRUCTIONS:

1. **Prepare the Dough:**
- In a large mixing bowl, combine the sourdough discard, flour, warm water, melted butter, sugar, salt, and instant yeast (if using). Mix until a rough dough forms.
2. **Kneading:**
- Turn the dough out onto a lightly floured surface and knead for about 8-10 minutes until it becomes smooth and elastic. If the dough is too sticky, add a little more flour as needed.
3. **First Rise:**
- Place the dough back into the mixing bowl, cover it with a clean kitchen towel or plastic wrap, and let it rise at room temperature for 3-4 hours, or until it has doubled in size.
4. **Shaping:**
- Once the dough has risen, turn it out onto a lightly floured surface and divide it into 12 equal pieces. Shape each piece into a ball by pulling the edges under and pinching them together at the bottom to create a smooth top.
5. **Second Rise:**
- Place the shaped rolls on a baking sheet lined with parchment paper or a silicone baking mat. Cover with a clean kitchen towel and let them rise for another 1-2 hours, or until they have doubled in size.
6. **Preheat the Oven:**
- About 30 minutes before baking, preheat your oven to 375°F (190°C).
7. **Baking:**
- Place the baking sheet in the preheated oven and bake for 20-25 minutes, or until the rolls are golden brown and sound hollow when tapped on the bottom.
8. **Cooling:**
- Remove the golden rolls from the oven and let them cool on a wire rack for at least 10 minutes before serving.
9. **Serving:**
- Serve the golden rolls warm or at room temperature. They can be enjoyed plain, with butter, or as a side for any meal.
10. **Storage:**
- Store any leftover golden rolls in an airtight container at room temperature for up to 2 days. For longer storage, freeze the rolls and reheat in the oven before serving.

CIABATTA

Calories 130; Fat 1 g; Carb 26 g; Protein 5 g

SERVINGS:
2

| PREP TIME:230 minutes | RISING TIME: 12-18 hours | BAKING TIME: 20-25 minutes |

UTENSILS:

- Large mixing bowl
- Measuring cups and spoons
- Kitchen scale
- Clean kitchen towel or plastic wrap
- Baking sheet
- Parchment paper or silicone baking mat
- Bench scraper or sharp knife

INGREDIENTS:

- 1 cup (8 oz) sourdough discard
- 3 1/4 cups (14.5 oz) bread flour
- 1 1/4 cups (10 oz) water, room temperature
- 2 tablespoons olive oil
- 2 teaspoons salt
- 1/2 teaspoon instant yeast (optional, for a quicker rise)

INSTRUCTIONS:

1. **Prepare the Dough:**
- In a large mixing bowl, combine the sourdough discard, bread flour, water, olive oil, salt, and instant yeast (if using). Mix until a rough dough forms. The dough will be very sticky and wet.

2. **First Rise (Bulk Fermentation):**
- Cover the mixing bowl with a clean kitchen towel or plastic wrap and let it rise at room temperature for 3-4 hours. Then transfer the dough to the refrigerator to ferment overnight (12-18 hours).

3. **Stretch and Fold:**
- The next morning, remove the dough from the refrigerator and let it come to room temperature. Perform 3 sets of stretch and folds, spaced 30 minutes apart. To stretch and fold, gently pull one side of the dough up and fold it over itself, then rotate the bowl and repeat on all sides.

4. **Shaping:**
- After the final stretch and fold, let the dough rest for 30 minutes. Turn the dough out onto a well-floured surface. Using a bench scraper or sharp knife, divide the dough into two equal pieces. Gently shape each piece into a rectangle, being careful not to deflate the dough.

5. **Second Rise:**
- Place the shaped dough on a baking sheet lined with parchment paper or a silicone baking mat. Cover with a clean kitchen towel and let it rise at room temperature for 2-3 hours, or until the dough has visibly puffed up.

6. **Preheat the Oven:**
- About 30 minutes before baking, preheat your oven to 475°F (245°C). Place a shallow pan of water on the bottom rack of the oven to create steam, which helps develop a crisp crust.

7. **Baking:**
- Dust the tops of the loaves with flour. Place the baking sheet in the preheated oven and bake for 20-25 minutes, or until the ciabatta is golden brown and sounds hollow when tapped on the bottom.

8. **Cooling:**
- Remove the ciabatta from the oven and let it cool on a wire rack for at least 30 minutes before slicing.

9. **Serving:**
- Serve the ciabatta as a sandwich bread, or enjoy it plain with olive oil and balsamic vinegar.

10. **Storage:**
- Store any leftover ciabatta in an airtight container at room temperature for up to 2 days. For longer storage, freeze the ciabatta and reheat in the oven before serving.

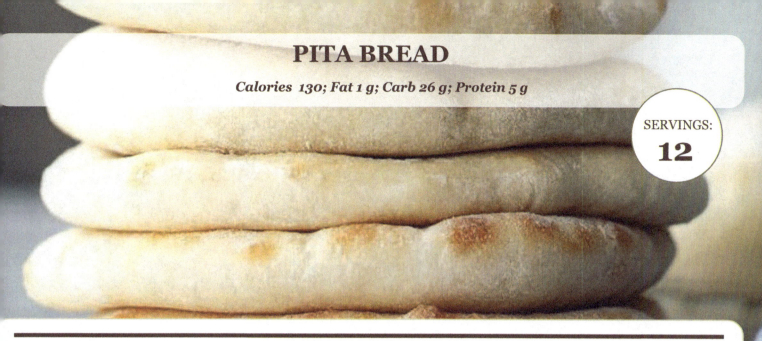

PITA BREAD

Calories 130; Fat 1 g; Carb 26 g; Protein 5 g

SERVINGS:
12

PREP TIME: 20 minutes   RISING TIME: 4-6 hours   BAKING TIME: 8-10 minutes

UTENSILS:

- Large mixing bowl
- Measuring cups and spoons
- Kitchen scale
- Clean kitchen towel or plastic wrap
- Baking sheet or pizza stone
- Rolling pin
- Clean kitchen towel

INGREDIENTS:

- 1 cup (8 oz) sourdough discard
- 3 cups (13.5 oz) all-purpose flour
- 1 cup (8 oz) warm water
- 2 tablespoons olive oil
- 2 teaspoons salt
- 1 teaspoon sugar
- 1 teaspoon instant yeast (optional, for a quicker rise)

INSTRUCTIONS:

1. **Prepare the Dough:**
- In a large mixing bowl, combine the sourdough discard, flour, warm water, olive oil, salt, sugar, and instant yeast (if using). Mix until a rough dough forms.
2. **Kneading:**
- Turn the dough out onto a lightly floured surface and knead for about 8-10 minutes until it becomes smooth and elastic. If the dough is too sticky, add a little more flour as needed.
3. **First Rise:**
- Place the dough back into the mixing bowl, cover it with a clean kitchen towel or plastic wrap, and let it rise at room temperature for 4-6 hours, or until it has doubled in size.
4. **Shaping:**
- Once the dough has risen, turn it out onto a lightly floured surface and divide it into 8 equal pieces. Shape each piece into a ball by pulling the edges under and pinching them together at the bottom to create a smooth top.
5. **Resting:**
- Cover the dough balls with a clean kitchen towel and let them rest for 10-15 minutes to relax the gluten.
6. **Rolling:**
- Using a rolling pin, roll each dough ball into a flat circle about 1/4 inch thick. Make sure they are evenly rolled to ensure proper puffing.
7. **Preheat the Oven:**
- While the dough is resting, preheat your oven to 475°F (245°C). If you have a pizza stone, place it in the oven to preheat as well. If not, you can use a baking sheet.
8. **Baking:**
- Place the rolled-out dough circles on the preheated pizza stone or baking sheet. Bake for 8-10 minutes, or until the pitas puff up and are lightly golden brown. You may need to bake in batches depending on the size of your oven and baking surface.
9. **Cooling:**
- Remove the pitas from the oven and place them on a clean kitchen towel. Cover with another kitchen towel to keep them soft as they cool.
10. **Serving:**
- Serve the pita bread warm or at room temperature. It can be enjoyed plain, with dips, or used for sandwiches and wraps.
11. **Storage:**
- Store any leftover pita bread in an airtight container at room temperature for up to 2 days. For longer storage, freeze the pitas and reheat in the oven or toaster before serving.

BRIOCHE

Calories 120; Fat 4 g; Carb 17 g; Protein 3 g

SERVINGS:
1

PREP TIME: 30 minutes | **RISING TIME:** 8-12 hours | **BAKING TIME:** 30-35 minutes

---

UTENSILS:

- Stand mixer with dough hook attachment (optional)
- Large mixing bowl
- Measuring cups and spoons
- Kitchen scale
- Clean kitchen towel or plastic wrap
- 9x5 inch loaf pan
- Parchment paper
- Pastry brush

INGREDIENTS:

- 1 cup (8 oz) sourdough discard
- 3 1/2 cups (15.75 oz) all-purpose flour
- 1/4 cup (2 oz) warm milk
- 3 large eggs, at room temperature
- 1/4 cup (2 oz) granulated sugar
- 1 teaspoon salt
- 1 tablespoon instant yeast (optional, for a quicker rise)
- 1 cup (8 oz) unsalted butter, softened and cut into pieces

Egg Wash:
- 1 egg
- 1 tablespoon water

INSTRUCTIONS:

1. **Prepare the Dough:**
- In the bowl of a stand mixer, combine the sourdough discard, flour, warm milk, eggs, sugar, salt, and instant yeast (if using). Mix on low speed until a rough dough forms, about 2-3 minutes. If mixing by hand, combine the ingredients in a large mixing bowl and stir until a rough dough forms.

2. **Kneading:**
- With the mixer on medium speed, add the softened butter a few pieces at a time, mixing until fully incorporated before adding more. Continue to knead the dough for about 10-15 minutes, until it is smooth and elastic. If kneading by hand, incorporate the butter gradually while kneading, and continue to knead until the dough is smooth and elastic.

3. **First Rise (Bulk Fermentation):**
- Transfer the dough to a large, lightly greased mixing bowl. Cover with a clean kitchen towel or plastic wrap and let it rise at room temperature for 4-6 hours. Then transfer the dough to the refrigerator to ferment overnight (8-12 hours).

4. **Shaping:**
- The next morning, remove the dough from the refrigerator and let it come to room temperature. Turn the dough out onto a lightly floured surface and gently deflate it. Shape the dough into a rectangle, then roll it tightly from the short end to form a log.

5. **Second Rise:**
- Place the shaped dough into a 9x5 inch loaf pan lined with parchment paper. Cover with a clean kitchen towel and let it rise at room temperature for 2-3 hours, or until it has doubled in size.

6. **Preheat the Oven:**
- About 30 minutes before baking, preheat your oven to 375°F (190°C).

7. **Egg Wash:**
- In a small bowl, whisk together the egg and water to make the egg wash. Brush the top of the risen loaf with the egg wash using a pastry brush.

8. **Baking:**
- Place the loaf pan in the preheated oven and bake for 30-35 minutes, or until the brioche is golden brown and sounds hollow when tapped on the bottom. If the top is browning too quickly, cover loosely with aluminum foil.

9. **Cooling:**
- Remove the brioche from the oven and let it cool in the pan for 10 minutes. Then transfer the loaf to a wire rack to cool completely before slicing.

10. **Serving:**
- Slice and serve the brioche as desired. It can be enjoyed plain, with butter, jam, or used for sandwiches and French toast.

11. **Storage:**
- Store any leftover brioche in an airtight container at room temperature for up to 3 days. For longer storage, freeze the brioche and reheat in the oven before serving.

CHALLAH

Calories 130; Fat 2 g; Carb 24 g; Protein 4 g

SERVINGS:
1

| PREP TIME: 30 minutes | RISING TIME: 8-12 hours | BAKING TIME: 25-30 minutes |

UTENSILS:

- Large mixing bowl
- Measuring cups and spoons
- Kitchen scale
- Clean kitchen towel or plastic wrap
- Baking sheet
- Parchment paper
- Pastry brush

INGREDIENTS:

- 1 cup (8 oz) sourdough discard
- 4 cups (17 oz) all-purpose flour
- 1/2 cup (4 oz) warm water
- 1/4 cup (2 oz) granulated sugar
- 1/4 cup (2 oz) vegetable oil
- 2 large eggs
- 2 teaspoons salt
- 1 tablespoon instant yeast (optional, for a quicker rise)

Egg Wash:
- 1 egg
- 1 tablespoon water
- Poppy seeds or sesame seeds for sprinkling (optional)

INSTRUCTIONS:

1. **Prepare the Dough:**
- In a large mixing bowl, combine the sourdough discard, flour, warm water, sugar, vegetable oil, eggs, salt, and instant yeast (if using). Mix until a rough dough forms.
2. **Kneading:**
- Turn the dough out onto a lightly floured surface and knead for about 8-10 minutes until it becomes smooth and elastic. If the dough is too sticky, add a little more flour as needed.
3. **First Rise (Bulk Fermentation):**
- Place the dough back into the mixing bowl, cover it with a clean kitchen towel or plastic wrap, and let it rise at room temperature for 4-6 hours. Then transfer the dough to the refrigerator to ferment overnight (8-12 hours).
4. **Shaping:**
- The next morning, remove the dough from the refrigerator and let it come to room temperature. Turn the dough out onto a lightly floured surface and divide it into three equal pieces. Roll each piece into a long rope, about 18 inches in length.
5. **Braiding:**
- Pinch the ends of the three ropes together and braid them, pinching the ends together and tucking them under the loaf to seal.
6. **Second Rise:**
- Place the braided loaf on a baking sheet lined with parchment paper. Cover with a clean kitchen towel and let it rise at room temperature for 2-3 hours, or until it has doubled in size.
7. **Preheat the Oven:**
- About 30 minutes before baking, preheat your oven to 375°F (190°C).
8. **Egg Wash:**
- In a small bowl, whisk together the egg and water to make the egg wash. Brush the top of the risen loaf with the egg wash using a pastry brush. Sprinkle with poppy seeds or sesame seeds if desired.
9. **Baking:**
- Place the baking sheet in the preheated oven and bake for 25-30 minutes, or until the challah is golden brown and sounds hollow when tapped on the bottom. If the top is browning too quickly, cover loosely with aluminum foil.
10. **Cooling:**
- Remove the challah from the oven and let it cool on a wire rack for at least 30 minutes before slicing.
11. **Serving:**
- Slice and serve the challah as desired. It can be enjoyed plain, with butter, or used for sandwiches and French toast.
12. **Storage:**
- Store any leftover challah in an airtight container at room temperature for up to 3 days. For longer storage, freeze the challah and reheat in the oven before serving.

SNACKS & APPETIZERS

CRACKERS

Calories 120; Fat 4 g; Carb 20 g; Protein 2 g

SERVINGS:

2

PREP TIME: 15 minutes	RISING TIME: 30 minutes	BAKING TIME: 20-25 minutes

UTENSILS:

- Large mixing bowl
- Measuring cups and spoons
- Kitchen scale
- Rolling pin
- Baking sheet
- Parchment paper or silicone baking mat
- Pizza cutter or sharp knife

INGREDIENTS:

- 1 cup (8 oz) sourdough discard
- 1 cup (4.5 oz) all-purpose flour
- 1/4 cup (2 oz) olive oil
- 1/2 teaspoon salt
- 1/2 teaspoon garlic powder (optional)
- 1/2 teaspoon dried herbs (such as rosemary, thyme, or oregano) (optional)
- Coarse sea salt, for sprinkling

INSTRUCTIONS:

1. **Prepare the Dough:**
- In a large mixing bowl, combine the sourdough discard, flour, olive oil, salt, garlic powder, and dried herbs (if using). Mix until a rough dough forms.
2. **Resting:**
- Cover the dough with a clean kitchen towel or plastic wrap and let it rest for 30 minutes. This allows the flour to hydrate and makes the dough easier to roll out.
3. **Preheat the Oven:**
- Preheat your oven to 350°F (175°C). Line two baking sheets with parchment paper or silicone baking mats.
4. **Rolling:**
- Divide the dough into two equal pieces. On a lightly floured surface, roll out one piece of dough as thin as possible, aiming for about 1/8 inch thickness. The thinner the dough, the crispier the crackers will be.
5. **Cutting:**
- Transfer the rolled-out dough to a prepared baking sheet. Use a pizza cutter or sharp knife to cut the dough into desired cracker shapes (squares, rectangles, or triangles). You can also use a fork to poke holes in each cracker to prevent them from puffing up during baking.
6. **Seasoning:**
- Lightly brush the dough with olive oil and sprinkle with coarse sea salt.
7. **Baking:**
- Bake in the preheated oven for 20-25 minutes, or until the crackers are golden brown and crisp. Keep an eye on them, as thinner crackers may bake more quickly.
8. **Cooling:**
- Remove the crackers from the oven and let them cool on a wire rack. They will continue to crisp up as they cool.
9. **Repeat:**
- Repeat the rolling, cutting, and baking process with the remaining piece of dough.
10. **Serving:**
- Serve the crackers plain or with your favorite dips, cheeses, or spreads.
11. **Storage:**
- Store any leftover crackers in an airtight container at room temperature for up to 1 week.

CHEESE STRAWS

Calories 80; Fat 5 g; Carb 6 g; Protein 2 g

SERVINGS:
24

| PREP TIME: 20 minutes | RISING TIME: 30 minutes | BAKING TIME: 15-18 minutes |

UTENSILS:

- Large mixing bowl
- Measuring cups and spoons
- Kitchen scale
- Rolling pin
- Baking sheet
- Parchment paper or silicone baking mat
- Sharp knife or pizza cutter
- Pastry brush

INGREDIENTS:

- 1 cup (8 oz) sourdough discard
- 1 1/2 cups (6.75 oz) all-purpose flour
- 1/2 cup (4 oz) unsalted butter, cold and cubed
- 1 1/2 cups (6 oz) sharp cheddar cheese, grated
- 1/2 teaspoon salt
- 1/2 teaspoon garlic powder (optional)
- 1/2 teaspoon paprika (optional)
- 1/4 teaspoon cayenne pepper (optional, for a bit of heat)
- 1 egg, beaten (for egg wash)

INSTRUCTIONS:

1. **Prepare the Dough:**
- In a large mixing bowl, combine the sourdough discard, flour, cold cubed butter, grated cheddar cheese, salt, garlic powder, paprika, and cayenne pepper (if using). Mix until a rough dough forms. You can use a pastry cutter or your fingers to incorporate the butter into the flour mixture until it resembles coarse crumbs.
2. **Chilling:**
- Turn the dough out onto a lightly floured surface and shape it into a disk. Wrap it in plastic wrap and refrigerate for at least 30 minutes to firm up.
3. **Preheat the Oven:**
- Preheat your oven to 375°F (190°C). Line a baking sheet with parchment or a silicone baking mat.
4. **Rolling:**
- On a lightly floured surface, roll out the chilled dough into a rectangle about 1/8 inch thick.
5. **Cutting:**
- Use a sharp knife or pizza cutter to cut the dough into long strips, about 1/2 inch wide and 6-8 inches long.
6. **Twisting:**
- Gently twist each strip several times and place them on the prepared baking sheet, spacing them about 1 inch apart.
7. **Egg Wash:**
- Brush the twisted dough strips with the beaten egg using a pastry brush. This will give the cheese straws a nice golden color when baked.
8. **Baking:**
- Bake in the preheated oven for 15-18 minutes, or until the cheese straws are golden brown and crisp.
9. **Cooling:**
- Remove the cheese straws from the oven and let them cool on a wire rack.
10. **Serving:**
- Serve the cheese straws as a snack or appetizer. They are delicious on their own or with dips.
11. **Storage:**
- Store any leftover cheese straws in an airtight container at room temperature for up to 3 days.

GARLIC KNOTS

Calories 150; Fat 5 g; Carb 21 g; Protein 4 g

SERVINGS:
12

PREP TIME: 20 minutes   **RISING TIME:** 4-6 hours   **BAKING TIME:** 15-20 minutes

UTENSILS:

- Large mixing bowl
- Measuring cups and spoons
- Kitchen scale
- Clean kitchen towel or plastic wrap
- Baking sheet
- Parchment paper or silicone baking mat
- Pastry brush
- Small saucepan

INGREDIENTS:

- 1 cup (8 oz) sourdough discard
- 3 cups (13.5 oz) all-purpose flour
- 3/4 cup (6 oz) warm water
- 1/4 cup (2 oz) olive oil
- 2 tablespoons granulated sugar
- 1 1/2 teaspoons salt
- 1 teaspoon instant yeast (optional, for a quicker rise)

Garlic Butter:
- 1/4 cup (2 oz) unsalted butter
- 2 tablespoons olive oil
- 4 cloves garlic, minced
- 2 tablespoons fresh parsley, chopped (optional)
- 1/2 teaspoon salt

INSTRUCTIONS:

1. **Prepare the Dough:**
- In a large mixing bowl, combine the sourdough discard, flour, warm water, olive oil, sugar, salt, and instant yeast (if using). Mix until a rough dough forms.
2. **Kneading:**
- Turn the dough out onto a lightly floured surface and knead for about 8-10 minutes until it becomes smooth and elastic. If the dough is too sticky, add a little more flour as needed.
3. **First Rise:**
- Place the dough back into the mixing bowl, cover it with a clean kitchen towel or plastic wrap, and let it rise at room temperature for 4-6 hours, or until it has doubled in size.
4. **Shaping:**
- Once the dough has risen, turn it out onto a lightly floured surface. Divide the dough into 12 equal pieces. Roll each piece into a rope about 6-8 inches long and tie each rope into a knot.
5. **Second Rise:**
- Place the shaped knots on a baking sheet lined with parchment paper or a silicone baking mat. Cover with a clean kitchen towel and let them rise for another 1-2 hours, or until they have puffed up slightly.
6. **Preheat the Oven:**
- About 30 minutes before baking, preheat your oven to 375°F (190°C).
7. **Prepare the Garlic Butter:**
- While the knots are rising, melt the butter with the olive oil in a small saucepan over low heat. Add the minced garlic and salt, and cook for 1-2 minutes until fragrant. Remove from heat and stir in the chopped parsley, if using.
8. **Baking:**
- Bake the knots in the preheated oven for 15-20 minutes, or until they are golden brown.
9. **Brushing with Garlic Butter:**
- Remove the knots from the oven and immediately brush them generously with the garlic butter.
10. **Serving:**
- Serve the garlic knots warm. They are perfect on their own or as a side to pasta, soup, or salad.
11. **Storage:**
- Store any leftover garlic knots in an airtight container at room temperature for up to 2 days. For longer storage, freeze the knots and reheat in the oven before serving.

VEGETABLE FRITTERS

Calories 100; Fat 4 g; Carb 12 g; Protein 2 g

SERVINGS: 15

PREP TIME: 15 minutes

COOKING TIME: 10-12 minutes

UTENSILS:

- Large mixing bowl
- Measuring cups and spoons
- Kitchen scale
- Whisk
- Large skillet or frying pan
- Slotted spoon
- Paper towels

INGREDIENTS:

- 1 cup (8 oz) sourdough discard
- 1 cup (4.5 oz) all-purpose flour
- 1/2 cup (4 oz) milk or water
- 1 large egg
- 1 teaspoon baking powder
- 1/2 teaspoon salt
- 1/2 teaspoon black pepper
- 1 cup vegetables, finely chopped (such as zucchini, corn, bell pepper, or spinach)
- 1/2 cup grated cheese (optional)
- 2 tablespoons chopped fresh herbs (such as parsley, chives, or dill)
- Oil for frying (vegetable oil or olive oil)

INSTRUCTIONS:

1. **Prepare the Batter:**
- In a large mixing bowl, whisk together the sourdough, discarding it, flour, milk or water, egg, baking powder, salt, and black pepper until smooth and well combined.
2. **Add the Fillings:**
- Fold in the finely chopped vegetables, grated cheese (if using), and chopped fresh herbs until evenly distributed throughout the batter.
3. **Preheat the Oil:**
- Heat about 1/4 inch of oil in a large skillet or frying pan over medium heat until shimmering.
4. **Cooking the Fritters:**
- Using a spoon or small ladle, drop spoonfuls of batter into the hot oil, flattening them slightly with the back of the spoon. Fry the fritters in batches, making sure not to overcrowd the pan.
5. **Frying:**
- Cook the fritters for 2-3 minutes on each side, or until they are golden brown and crispy. Use a slotted spoon to transfer the cooked fritters to a plate lined with paper towels to drain any excess oil.
6. **Repeat:**
- Repeat the frying process with the remaining batter, adding more oil to the pan as needed.
7. **Serving:**
- Serve the fritters warm with your favorite dipping sauce, such as sour cream, tzatziki, or a spicy aioli.
8. **Storage:**
- Store any leftover fritters in an airtight container in the refrigerator for up to 2 days. Reheat in the oven or a skillet before serving.

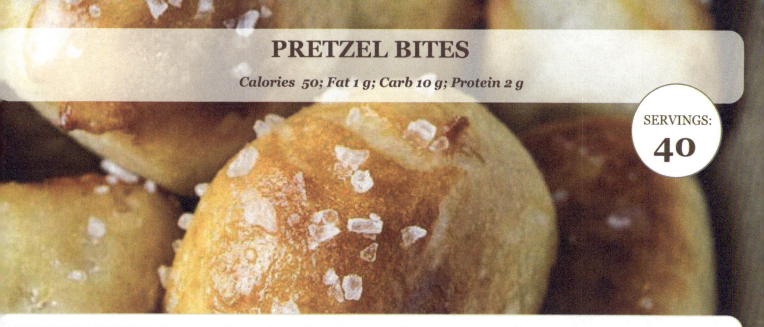

PRETZEL BITES

Calories 50; Fat 1 g; Carb 10 g; Protein 2 g

SERVINGS:
40

PREP TIME: 30 minutes   RISING TIME: 1-2 hours   BAKING TIME: 10-15 minutes

---

UTENSILS:

- Large mixing bowl
- Measuring cups and spoons
- Kitchen scale
- Clean kitchen towel or plastic wrap
- Baking sheet
- Parchment paper or silicone baking mat
- Large pot
- Slotted spoon
- Sharp knife or kitchen scissors
- Pastry brush

INGREDIENTS:

- 1 cup (8oz) sourdough discard
- 3 cups (13.5 oz) bread flour
- 1 cup (8 oz) warm water
- 2 tablespoons unsalted butter, melted
- 1 tablespoon granulated sugar
- 2 teaspoons salt
- 1 teaspoon instant yeast (optional, for a quicker rise)

For the boiling solution:
- 10 cups water
- 1/2 cup baking soda

Topping:
- Coarse sea salt, for sprinkling
- 1/4 cup (2 oz) unsalted butter, melted (for brushing after baking)

INSTRUCTIONS:

1. **Prepare the Dough:**
- In a large mixing bowl, combine the sourdough discard, bread flour, warm water, melted butter, sugar, salt, and instant yeast (if using). Mix until a rough dough forms.
2. **Kneading:**
- Turn the dough out onto a lightly floured surface and knead for about 8-10 minutes until it becomes smooth and elastic. If the dough is too sticky, add a little more flour as needed.
3. **First Rise:**
- Place the dough back into the mixing bowl, cover it with a clean kitchen towel or plastic wrap, and let it rise at room temperature for 1-2 hours, or until it has doubled in size.
4. **Shaping:**
- Once the dough has risen, turn it out onto a lightly floured surface. Divide the dough into 4 equal pieces. Roll each piece into a rope about 1/2 inch in diameter. Use a sharp knife or kitchen scissors to cut the ropes into 1-inch pieces.
5. **Preheat the Oven:**
- About 30 minutes before baking, preheat your oven to 425°F (220°C). Line a baking sheet with parchment or a silicone baking mat.
6. **Prepare the Boiling Solution:**
- In a large pot, bring 10 cups of water to a boil. Carefully add the baking soda to the boiling water.
7. **Boiling:**
- Using a slotted spoon, carefully lower the pretzel bites into the boiling water, a few at a time. Boil for about 30 seconds, then remove with the slotted spoon and place on the prepared baking sheet. Repeat with the remaining pretzel bites.
8. **Topping:**
- While the pretzel bites are still wet, sprinkle them with coarse sea salt.
9. **Baking:**
- Bake in the preheated oven for 10-15 minutes, or until the pretzel bites are deep golden brown.
10. **Brushing with Butter:**
- Remove the pretzel bites from the oven and immediately brush them with melted butter.
11. **Serving:**
- Serve the pretzel bites warm with your favorite dipping sauces, such as mustard, cheese sauce, or marinara.
12. **Storage:**
- Store any leftover pretzel bites in an airtight container at room temperature for up to 2 days. For longer storage, freeze the bites and reheat in the oven before serving.

SAVORY MUFFINS

Calories 180; Fat 8 g; Carb 22 g; Protein 5 g

SERVINGS:
12

PREP TIME: 15 minutes

COOKING TIME: 20-25 minutes

UTENSILS:

- Large mixing bowl
- Medium mixing bowl
- Measuring cups and spoons
- Muffin tin
- Paper muffin liners or non-stick cooking spray
- Whisk
- Spoon or spatula

INGREDIENTS:

- 1 cup (8 oz) sourdough discard
- 1 cup (4.5 oz) all-purpose flour
- 1/2 cup (2 oz) whole wheat flour (optional for extra flavor and nutrition)
- 1/2 cup (4 oz) milk
- 1/4 cup (2 oz) olive oil or melted butter
- 2 large eggs
- 1/2 cup (2 oz) shredded cheese (cheddar, parmesan, or your favorite)
- 1/2 cup (2 oz) chopped vegetables (such as bell peppers, spinach, or zucchini)
- 1/4 cup (1 oz) chopped green onions or chives
- 1 teaspoon baking powder
- 1/2 teaspoon baking soda
- 1/2 teaspoon salt
- 1/4 teaspoon black pepper
- 1/2 teaspoon dried herbs (such as oregano, thyme, or rosemary)

INSTRUCTIONS:

1. **Preheat the Oven:**
- Preheat your oven to 375°F (190°C). Line a muffin tin with paper liners or lightly grease with non-stick cooking spray.
2. **Prepare the Wet Ingredients:**
- In a large mixing bowl, whisk together the sourdough discard, milk, olive oil or melted butter, and eggs until well combined.
3. **Mix the Dry Ingredients:**
- In a medium mixing bowl, whisk together the all-purpose flour, whole wheat flour (if using), baking powder, baking soda, salt, black pepper, and dried herbs.
4. **Combine Wet and Dry Ingredients:**
- Gradually add the dry ingredients to the wet mixture, stirring until just combined. Be careful not to overmix; the batter should be slightly lumpy.
5. **Add Cheese and Vegetables:**
- Gently fold in the shredded cheese, chopped vegetables, and green onions or chives until evenly distributed throughout the batter.
6. **Fill the Muffin Tin:**
- Using a spoon or a 1/4 cup measuring cup, evenly distribute the batter into the prepared muffin tin, filling each cup about 2/3 full.
7. **Baking:**
- Place the muffin tin in the preheated oven and bake for 20-25 minutes, or until the muffins are golden brown and a toothpick inserted into the center comes out clean.
8. **Cooling:**
- Allow the muffins to cool in the tin for about 5 minutes before transferring them to a wire rack to cool completely.
9. **Serving:**
- Serve the savory muffins warm or at room temperature. They are perfect for breakfast, brunch, or as a snack.
10. **Storage:**
- Store any leftover muffins in an airtight container at room temperature for up to 3 days. They can also be frozen for longer storage. Reheat in the microwave or oven before serving.

BRUSCHETTA WITH TOMATOES

Calories 70; Fat 3 g; Carb 10 g; Protein 2 g

PREP TIME: 20 minutes   **COOKING TIME:** 10 minutes

UTENSILS:

- Large mixing bowl
- Measuring cups and spoons
- Kitchen scale
- Baking sheet
- Parchment paper or silicone baking mat
- Sharp knife
- Cutting board

INGREDIENTS:

- 1 cup (8 oz) sourdough discard
- 1 cup (4.5 oz) all-purpose flour
- 1/2 cup (4 oz) water
- 1/2 teaspoon salt
- 2 tablespoons olive oil
- 2-3 cloves garlic, minced
- 1 pint cherry tomatoes, diced
- 1/4 cup fresh basil, chopped
- 1 tablespoon balsamic vinegar
- Salt and pepper to taste
- Extra olive oil for brushing
- Optional: 1/4 cup grated Parmesan cheese

INSTRUCTIONS:

1. **Prepare the Sourdough Bruschetta Base:**
- In a large mixing bowl, combine the sourdough discard, all-purpose flour, water, and 1/2 teaspoon salt. Mix until a smooth batter forms.
2. **Preheat the Oven:**
- Preheat your oven to 425°F (220°C). Line a baking sheet with parchment or a silicone baking mat.
3. **Bake the Bruschetta Base:**
- Pour the batter onto the prepared baking sheet and spread it out evenly to form a thin layer. Bake in the preheated oven for 10-12 minutes, or until the base is golden brown and crispy.
4. **Prepare the Topping:**
- While the bruschetta base is baking, combine the diced cherry tomatoes, minced garlic, chopped basil, olive oil, balsamic vinegar, salt, and pepper in a large mixing bowl. Mix well and set aside.
5. **Assembly:**
- Once the bruschetta base is baked and crispy, remove it from the oven and let it cool slightly. Cut it into bite-sized pieces or desired shapes using a sharp knife or pizza cutter.
6. **Top the Bruschetta:**
- Spoon the tomato mixture onto each piece of the sourdough bruschetta base. If desired, sprinkle grated Parmesan cheese on top.
7. **Serving:**
- Arrange the bruschetta on a serving platter and serve immediately as an appetizer or snack.
8. **Storage:**
- The topping can be stored separately in an airtight container in the refrigerator for up to 2 days. Assemble the bruschetta just before serving to keep the base crispy.

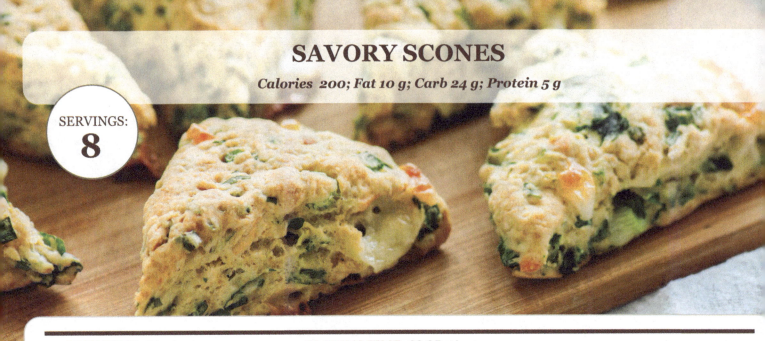

SAVORY SCONES

Calories 200; Fat 10 g; Carb 24 g; Protein 5 g

SERVINGS: 8

PREP TIME: 15 minutes   COOKING TIME: 20-25 minutes

UTENSILS:

- Large mixing bowl
- Measuring cups and spoons
- Kitchen scale
- Pastry cutter or forks
- Baking sheet
- Parchment paper or silicone baking mat
- Rolling pin (optional)
- Sharp knife or pastry cutter

INGREDIENTS:

- 1 cup (8 oz) sourdough discard
- 2 cups (9 oz) all-purpose flour
- 1 tablespoon baking powder
- 1/2 teaspoon baking soda
- 1 teaspoon salt
- 1/2 cup (4 oz) cold unsalted butter, cubed
- 1/2 cup (2 oz) grated sharp cheddar cheese
- 1/4 cup (1 oz) grated Parmesan cheese
- 1/4 cup chopped fresh herbs (such as chives, parsley, or thyme)
- 1/2 cup (4 oz) buttermilk or regular milk
- 1 large egg, beaten (for egg wash)
- Optional: 1/4 teaspoon black pepper or red pepper flakes for a kick

INSTRUCTIONS:

1. **Preheat the Oven:**
- Preheat your oven to 400°F (200°C). Line a baking sheet with parchment or a silicone baking mat.
2. **Prepare the Dry Ingredients:**
- In a large mixing bowl, whisk together the flour, baking powder, baking soda, and salt.
3. **Cut in the Butter:**
- Add the cold, cubed butter to the dry ingredients. Use a pastry cutter or forks to cut the butter into the flour mixture until it resembles coarse crumbs.
4. **Add the Cheese and Herbs:**
- Gently fold in the grated cheddar cheese, grated Parmesan cheese, and chopped fresh herbs. If you like a bit of heat, add black pepper or red pepper flakes.
5. **Combine Wet Ingredients:**
- In a separate bowl, mix the sourdough discard and buttermilk until well combined.
6. **Form the Dough:**
- Gradually add the wet mixture to the dry ingredients, stirring until just combined. Be careful not to overmix; the dough should be slightly sticky and shaggy.
7. **Shaping the Scones:**
- Turn the dough out onto a lightly floured surface. Gently knead it a few times to bring it together. Pat or roll the dough into a circle about 1 inch thick. Use a sharp knife or pastry cutter to cut the dough into 8 wedges.
8. **Prepare for Baking:**
- Place the scones on the prepared baking sheet. Brush the tops with the beaten egg for a shiny finish.
9. **Baking:**
- Bake in the preheated oven for 20-25 minutes, or until the scones are golden brown and a toothpick inserted into the center comes out clean.
10. **Cooling:**
- Allow the scones to cool on the baking sheet for a few minutes before transferring them to a wire rack to cool completely.
11. **Serving:**
- Serve the savory scones warm or at room temperature. They are perfect on their own, with butter, or alongside soups and salads.
12. **Storage:**
- Store any leftover scones in an airtight container at room temperature for up to 2 days. They can also be frozen for longer storage. Reheat in the oven or microwave before serving.

FLATBREAD

Calories 150; Fat 2 g; Carb 24 g; Protein 4 g

SERVINGS: 6

PREP TIME: 20 minutes   COOKING TIME: 10-15 minutes   TIME FOR THE REST: 30 minutes

UTENSILS:

- Large mixing bowl
- Measuring cups and spoons
- Kitchen scale
- Rolling pin
- Baking sheet or griddle
- Parchment paper (optional)
- Pastry brush

INGREDIENTS:

- 1 cup (8 oz) sourdough discard
- 1 1/2 cups (6.75 oz) all-purpose flour
- 1/2 cup (4 oz) water
- 2 tablespoons olive oil
- 1 teaspoon salt
- 1/2 teaspoon baking powder
- Optional toppings: olive oil, garlic, herbs, sesame seeds, za'atar, or other desired toppings

INSTRUCTIONS:

1. **Prepare the Dough:**
- In a large mixing bowl, combine the sourdough discard, flour, water, olive oil, salt, and baking powder. Mix until a rough dough forms.
2. **Kneading:**
- Turn the dough out onto a lightly floured surface and knead for about 5 minutes until it becomes smooth and elastic. If the dough is too sticky, add a little more flour as needed.
3. **Resting:**
- Place the dough back in the mixing bowl, cover it with a clean kitchen towel, and let it rest for about 30 minutes. This allows the gluten to relax and makes the dough easier to roll out.
4. **Preheat the Oven or Griddle:**
- If using an oven, preheat it to 475°F (246°C) and place a baking sheet inside to heat. If using a griddle, preheat it over medium-high heat.
5. **Shaping:**
- Divide the dough into 4-6 equal pieces. On a lightly floured surface, roll each piece into a thin round or oval shape, about 1/4 inch thick.
6. **Cooking the Flatbread:**
- If using an oven, place the rolled-out dough on the preheated baking sheet and bake for 8-10 minutes, or until the flatbread is puffed and golden brown. If using a griddle, cook each flatbread for about 2-3 minutes on each side, until golden brown and cooked through.
7. **Adding Toppings (Optional):**
- If desired, brush the warm flatbreads with olive oil and sprinkle with garlic, herbs, sesame seeds, za'atar, or other desired toppings.
8. **Serving:**
- Serve the flatbreads warm. They can be enjoyed plain, used as a base for pizzas, or served alongside dips and spreads.
9. **Storage:**
- Store any leftover flatbreads in an airtight container at room temperature for up to 2 days. For longer storage, freeze the flatbreads and reheat in the oven or on a griddle before serving.

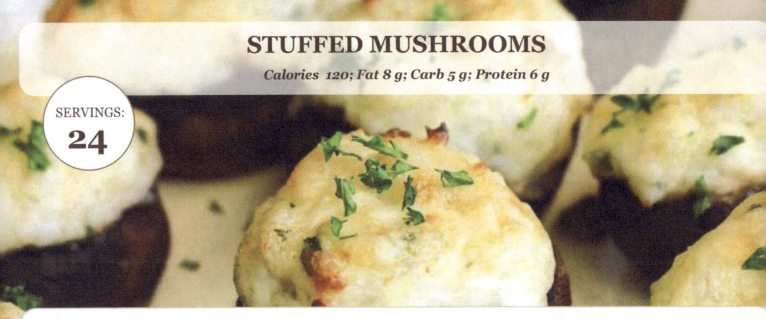

STUFFED MUSHROOMS

Calories 120; Fat 8 g; Carb 5 g; Protein 6 g

SERVINGS:
24

PREP TIME: 20 minutes   COOKING TIME: 30 minutes

UTENSILS:

- Large mixing bowl
- Measuring cups and spoons
- Baking sheet
- Parchment paper or silicone baking mat
- Sharp knife
- Cutting board
- Medium skillet

INGREDIENTS:

- 3 slices fresh sourdough bread, finely crumbled
- 22 oz large button mushrooms (about 24 mushrooms)
- 2 tablespoons butter
- 1 small to medium white onion, finely chopped
- 1/4 cup finely chopped celery
- 1/2 teaspoon ground oregano
- 1/4 teaspoon salt
- 1/8 teaspoon black pepper
- 1/2 cup grated aged Parmesan cheese

INSTRUCTIONS:

1. **Prepare the Mushrooms:**
- Preheat your oven to 375°F (190°C). Line a baking sheet with parchment or a silicone baking mat.
- Clean the mushrooms with a damp paper towel. Remove the stems and finely chop them. Set the mushroom caps aside.
2. **Prepare the Filling:**
- In a medium skillet, melt the butter over medium heat. Add the chopped onion and celery and sauté until softened, about 5 minutes.
- Add the chopped mushroom stems to the skillet and continue to cook for another 3-4 minutes until the mixture is tender.
- Stir in the ground oregano, salt, and black pepper. Remove from heat.
3. **Combine Ingredients:**
- In a large mixing bowl, combine the sautéed vegetable mixture, sourdough bread crumbs and grated Parmesan cheese. Mix until well combined.
4. **Stuff the Mushrooms:**
- Using a spoon, fill each mushroom cap with the stuffing mixture, pressing it down slightly to ensure it's well-packed.
5. **Baking:**
- Arrange the stuffed mushrooms on the prepared baking sheet. Bake in the preheated oven for 20-25 minutes, or until the mushrooms are tender and the tops are golden brown.
6. **Serving:**
- Serve the stuffed mushrooms warm as an appetizer or side dish. They are perfect for parties or as a delicious starter for any meal.
7. **Storage:**
- Store any leftover stuffed mushrooms in an airtight container in the refrigerator for up to 2 days. Reheat in the oven before serving.

LUNCH & DINNER

PIZZA CRUST

Calories 150; Fat 2 g; Carb 28 g; Protein 5 g

| PREP TIME: 20 minutes | RISING TIME: 4-6 hours | BAKING TIME: 10-15 minutes |

UTENSILS:

- Large mixing bowl
- Measuring cups and spoons
- Kitchen scale
- Clean kitchen towel or plastic wrap
- Baking sheet or pizza stone
- Parchment paper (optional)
- Rolling pin

INGREDIENTS:

- 1 cup (8 oz) sourdough discard
- 3 cups (13.5 oz) bread flour
- 1 cup (8 oz) warm water
- 2 tablespoons olive oil
- 2 teaspoons salt
- 1 teaspoon sugar
- 1 teaspoon instant yeast (optional, for a quicker rise)

INSTRUCTIONS:

1. **Prepare the Dough:**
- In a large mixing bowl, combine the sourdough discard, bread flour, warm water, olive oil, salt, sugar, and instant yeast (if using). Mix until a rough dough forms.
2. **Kneading:**
- Turn the dough out onto a lightly floured surface and knead for about 8-10 minutes until it becomes smooth and elastic. If the dough is too sticky, add a little more flour as needed.
3. **First Rise:**
- Place the dough back into the mixing bowl, cover it with a clean kitchen towel or plastic wrap, and let it rise at room temperature for 4-6 hours, or until it has doubled in size.
4. **Preheat the Oven:**
- About 30 minutes before baking, preheat your oven to 475°F (245°C). If using a pizza stone, place it in the oven to preheat. When using a baking sheet, cover it with parchment or lightly grease it.
5. **Shaping the Dough:**
- Once the dough has risen, turn it out onto a lightly floured surface. Divide the dough into two equal pieces. Shape each piece into a ball and let them rest for 10 minutes.
6. **Rolling the Dough:**
- Roll each dough ball into a circle or rectangle, about 1/4 inch thick. Transfer the rolled-out dough to a piece of parchment paper if using a pizza stone, or directly onto the prepared baking sheet.
7. **Topping the Pizza:**
- Add your desired toppings to the pizza crusts. Start with a layer of sauce, followed by cheese, meats, vegetables, and any other toppings you like.
8. **Baking:**
- If using a pizza stone, slide the parchment paper with the pizza onto the preheated stone. If using a baking sheet, place it in the preheated oven. Bake for 10-15 minutes, or until the crust is golden brown and the cheese is bubbly and melted.
9. **Serving:**
- Remove the pizzas from the oven and let them cool for a few minutes before slicing and serving.
10. **Storage:**
- Store any leftover pizza in an airtight container in the refrigerator for up to 2 days. Reheat in the oven or microwave before serving.

CALZONES WITH CHEESE AND PEPPERONI

Calories 550; Fat 25 g; Carb 65 g; Protein 30 g

SERVINGS:
4

PREP TIME: 30 minutes   **RISING TIME:** 4-6 hours   **BAKING TIME:** 20-25 minutes

UTENSILS:

- Large mixing bowl
- Measuring cups and spoons
- Kitchen scale
- Clean kitchen towel or plastic wrap
- Baking sheet
- Parchment paper or silicone baking mat
- Rolling pin
- Pastry brush
- Sharp knife or kitchen scissors

INGREDIENTS:

- 1 cup (8 oz) sourdough discard
- 3 cups (13.5 oz) bread flour
- 1 cup (8 oz) warm water
- 2 tablespoons olive oil
- 2 teaspoons salt
- 1 teaspoon sugar
- 1 teaspoon instant yeast (optional, for a quicker rise)

Filling:
- 1 cup ricotta cheese
- 1 cup shredded mozzarella cheese
- 1/2 cup grated Parmesan cheese
- 1/2 cup cooked and crumbled Italian sausage or diced pepperoni
- 1/2 cup sautéed vegetables (such as bell peppers, mushrooms, or spinach)
- 1 teaspoon dried oregano
- 1 teaspoon dried basil
- Salt and pepper to taste

Egg Wash:
- 1 egg, beaten
- 1 tablespoon water

INSTRUCTIONS:

1. **Prepare the Dough:**
- In a large mixing bowl, combine the sourdough discard, bread flour, warm water, olive oil, salt, sugar, and instant yeast (if using). Mix until a rough dough forms.
2. **Kneading:**
- Turn the dough out onto a lightly floured surface and knead for about 8-10 minutes until it becomes smooth and elastic. If the dough is too sticky, add a little more flour as needed.
3. **First Rise:**
- Place the dough back into the mixing bowl, cover it with a clean kitchen towel or plastic wrap, and let it rise at room temperature for 4-6 hours, or until it has doubled in size.
4. **Prepare the Filling:**
- In a medium mixing bowl, combine the ricotta cheese, shredded mozzarella cheese, grated Parmesan cheese, cooked sausage or pepperoni, sautéed vegetables, dried oregano, dried basil, salt, and pepper. Mix until well combined.
5. **Preheat the Oven:**
- About 30 minutes before baking, preheat your oven to 375°F (190°C). Line a baking sheet with parchment paper or a silicone baking mat.
6. **Shaping the Calzones:**
- Once the dough has risen, turn it out onto a lightly floured surface. Divide the dough into 4 equal pieces. Roll each piece into a circle about 8-10 inches in diameter.
7. **Filling the Calzones:**
- Place a generous amount of filling on one half of each dough circle, leaving a 1-inch border around the edges. Fold the other half of the dough over the filling to create a half-moon shape. Press the edges together to seal, then crimp the edges with a fork.
8. **Egg Wash:**
- In a small bowl, whisk together the beaten egg and water. Brush the tops of the calzones with the egg wash.
9. **Vent the Calzones:**
- Use a sharp knife or kitchen scissors to make a few small slits in the top of each calzone to allow steam to escape during baking.
10. **Baking:**
- Place the calzones on the prepared baking sheet and bake in the preheated oven for 20-25 minutes, or until they are golden brown and the filling is bubbly.
11. **Cooling:**
- Remove the calzones from the oven and let them cool on a wire rack for a few minutes before serving.
12. **Serving:**
- Serve the calzones warm with marinara sauce on the side for dipping.
13. **Storage:**
- Store any leftover calzones in an airtight container in the refrigerator for up to 2 days. Reheat in the oven or microwave before serving.

POT PIE

Calories 400; Fat 25 g; Carb 35 g; Protein 15 g

SERVINGS:
6

PREP TIME: 30 minutes   COOKING TIME: 45-50 minutes

UTENSILS:

- Large mixing bowl
- Measuring cups and spoons
- Kitchen scale
- Rolling pin
- Medium saucepan
- Large skillet
- Baking dish (9-inch pie dish or 2-quart baking dish)
- Pastry brush

INGREDIENTS:

Crust:
- 1 cup (8 oz) sourdough discard
- 1 1/2 cups (6.75 oz) all-purpose flour
- 1/2 cup (4 oz) cold unsalted butter, cubed
- 1/2 teaspoon salt
- 2-4 tablespoons cold water

Filling:
- 2 cups cooked chicken, diced (or turkey)
- 1 cup carrots, diced
- 1 cup peas (fresh or frozen)
- 1 cup potatoes, diced
- 1/2 cup celery, diced
- 1/2 cup onion, diced
- 3 tablespoons unsalted butter
- 1/4 cup all-purpose flour
- 2 cups chicken broth
- 1/2 cup milk or cream
- 1 teaspoon salt
- 1/2 teaspoon black pepper
- 1 teaspoon dried thyme
- 1 teaspoon dried rosemary

Egg Wash:
- 1 egg, beaten
- 1 tablespoon water

INSTRUCTIONS:

1. **Prepare the Crust:**
- In a large mixing bowl, combine the sourdough discard, flour, and salt. Add the cold, cubed butter and use a pastry cutter or your fingers to cut the butter into the flour mixture until it resembles coarse crumbs.
- Gradually add cold water, 1 tablespoon at a time, and mix until the dough comes together. Be careful not to overmix.
- Turn the dough out onto a lightly floured surface and shape it into a disk. Wrap it in plastic wrap and refrigerate for at least 30 minutes.

2. **Prepare the Filling:**
- In a medium saucepan, cook the diced potatoes in boiling water until tender, about 10 minutes. Drain and set aside.
- In a large skillet, melt the butter over medium heat. Add the onions, carrots, and celery, and cook until tender, about 5 minutes.
- Stir in the flour and cook for 1-2 minutes to create a roux.
- Gradually whisk in the chicken broth and milk, cooking and stirring until the mixture thickens, about 5 minutes.
- Add the cooked chicken, peas, cooked potatoes, salt, pepper, thyme, and rosemary. Stir to combine and remove from heat.

3. **Preheat the Oven:**
- Preheat your oven to 375°F (190°C).

4. **Assemble the Pot Pie:**
- Roll out the chilled dough on a lightly floured surface to fit your baking dish. If using a 9-inch pie dish, you can roll the dough into a circle. If using a 2-quart baking dish, roll it into a rectangle.
- Pour the filling into the baking dish. Place the rolled-out dough over the filling, trimming any excess and crimping the edges to seal.
- Cut a few small slits in the top crust to allow steam to escape.

5. **Egg Wash:**
- In a small bowl, whisk together the beaten egg and water. Brush the top crust with the egg wash.

6. **Baking:**
- Bake in the preheated oven for 45-50 minutes, or until the crust is golden brown and the filling is bubbly.

7. **Cooling:**
- Remove the pot pie from the oven and let it cool for about 10 minutes before serving.

8. **Serving:**
- Serve the pot pie warm. It's perfect for a comforting meal.

9. **Storage:**
- Store any leftover pot pie in an airtight container in the refrigerator for up to 3 days. Reheat in the oven or microwave before serving.

BEEF LASAGNA

Calories 350; Fat 20 g; Carb 25 g; Protein 20 g

SERVINGS: 12

PREP TIME: 45 minutes

BAKING TIME: 45-50 minutes

UTENSILS:

- Large mixing bowl
- Measuring cups and spoons
- Kitchen scale
- Large skillet
- Medium saucepan
- 9x13 inch baking dish
- Whisk
- Aluminum foil

INGREDIENTS:

Lasagna Noodles:
- 1 cup (8 oz) sourdough discard
- 2 cups (9 oz) all-purpose flour
- 1/2 teaspoon salt
- 2-3 large eggs
- 1-2 tablespoons water (as needed)

Meat Sauce:
- 1 pound ground beef or Italian sausage
- 1 small onion, diced
- 2 cloves garlic, minced
- 1 can (28 oz) crushed tomatoes
- 1 can (6 oz) tomato paste
- 1 can (15 oz) tomato sauce
- 2 tablespoons olive oil
- 1 teaspoon dried basil
- 1 teaspoon dried oregano
- 1/2 teaspoon salt
- 1/4 teaspoon black pepper
- 1 tablespoon sugar (optional)

Cheese Filling:
- 2 cups ricotta cheese
- 1/2 cup grated Parmesan cheese
- 1 large egg
- 2 tablespoons fresh parsley, chopped (or 1 tablespoon dried)
- 1/2 teaspoon salt
- 1/4 teaspoon black pepper

Additional Ingredients:
- 4 cups shredded mozzarella cheese

INSTRUCTIONS:

1. **Prepare the Lasagna Noodles:**
- In a large mixing bowl, combine the sourdough discard, flour, and salt. Make a well in the center and add the eggs. Mix until a dough forms, adding water as needed until the dough is smooth and elastic.
- Turn the dough out onto a lightly floured surface and knead for about 5 minutes until smooth. Cover with a clean towel and let rest for 30 minutes.
- Roll the dough out into thin sheets using a rolling pin or pasta machine. Cut into lasagna noodle lengths. Set aside.

2. **Prepare the Meat Sauce:**
- In a large skillet, heat the olive oil over medium heat. Add the diced onion and cook until softened, about 5 minutes. Add the minced garlic and cook for another minute.
- Add the ground beef or Italian sausage and cook until browned, breaking it up with a spoon as it cooks. Drain any excess fat.
- Stir in the crushed tomatoes, tomato paste, tomato sauce, dried basil, dried oregano, salt, black pepper, and sugar (if using). Simmer on low heat for 30 minutes, stirring occasionally.

3. **Prepare the Cheese Filling:**
- In a medium mixing bowl, combine the ricotta cheese, grated Parmesan cheese, egg, chopped parsley, salt, and black pepper. Mix well.

4. **Preheat the Oven:**
- Preheat your oven to 375°F (190°C).

5. **Assemble the Lasagna:**
- Spread a thin layer of meat sauce on the bottom of a 9x13 inch baking dish. Place a layer of lasagna noodles on top of the sauce.
- Spread a layer of the cheese filling over the noodles, followed by a layer of meat sauce. Sprinkle with a portion of shredded mozzarella cheese.
- Repeat the layers until all ingredients are used, ending with a layer of meat sauce and a generous amount of shredded mozzarella cheese on top.

6. **Baking:**
- Cover the baking dish with aluminum foil and bake in the preheated oven for 30 minutes. Remove the foil and bake for an additional 15-20 minutes, or until the cheese is bubbly and golden brown.

7. **Cooling:**
- Remove the lasagna from the oven and let it cool for about 10 minutes before slicing and serving.

8. **Serving:**
- Serve the lasagna warm with a side salad and garlic bread for a complete meal.

9. **Storage:**
- Store any leftover lasagna in an airtight container in the refrigerator for up to 3 days. Reheat in the oven or microwave before serving. Lasagna can also be frozen for longer storage.

TACOS

Calories 200; Fat 10 g; Carb 15 g; Protein 12 g

SERVINGS:
12

PREP TIME: 20 minutes | **TIME FOR THE REST: 30 minutes** | **COOKING TIME: 10-15 minutes**

UTENSILS:

- Large mixing bowl
- Measuring cups and spoons
- Kitchen scale
- Rolling pin
- Cast iron skillet or griddle
- Clean kitchen towel
- Tongs

INGREDIENTS:

Taco Tortillas:
- 1 cup (8 oz) sourdough discard
- 2 cups (9 oz) all-purpose flour
- 1/2 teaspoon salt
- 2 tablespoons olive oil
- 1/2 cup (4 oz) warm water

Taco Filling:
- 1 pound ground beef, chicken, or turkey
- 1 small onion, diced
- 2 cloves garlic, minced
- 1 tablespoon olive oil
- 1 tablespoon chili powder
- 1 teaspoon ground cumin
- 1 teaspoon paprika
- 1/2 teaspoon dried oregano
- 1/2 teaspoon salt
- 1/4 teaspoon black pepper
- 1/2 cup water or chicken broth

Toppings:
- Shredded lettuce
- Diced tomatoes
- Shredded cheese
- Sliced avocado
- Sour cream
- Salsa
- Fresh cilantro

INSTRUCTIONS:

1. **Prepare the Tortilla Dough:**
- In a large mixing bowl, combine the sourdough discard, flour, and salt. Add the olive oil and warm water. Mix until a dough forms.

2. **Kneading:**
- Turn the dough out onto a lightly floured surface and knead for about 5 minutes until smooth and elastic. If the dough is too sticky, add a little more flour as needed.

3. **Resting:**
- Place the dough back in the mixing bowl, cover it with a clean kitchen towel, and let it rest for 30 minutes. This allows the gluten to relax and makes the dough easier to roll out.

4. **Prepare the Taco Filling:**
- In a large skillet, heat the olive oil over medium heat. Add the diced onion and cook until softened, about 5 minutes. Add the minced garlic and cook for another minute.
- Add the ground meat and cook until browned, breaking it up with a spoon as it cooks. Drain any excess fat.
- Stir in the chili powder, ground cumin, paprika, dried oregano, salt, black pepper, and water or chicken broth. Simmer on low heat for 10 minutes, stirring occasionally. Remove from heat and set aside.

5. **Preheat the Skillet or Griddle:**
- Heat a cast iron skillet or griddle over medium-high heat.

6. **Shaping the Tortillas:**
- Divide the dough into 10-12 equal pieces. Roll each piece into a ball and then flatten it with a rolling pin into a thin circle, about 6-8 inches in diameter.

7. **Cooking the Tortillas:**
- Place each rolled-out dough circle onto the preheated skillet or griddle. Cook for about 1-2 minutes on each side, or until the tortilla is puffed and golden brown spots appear. Use tongs to flip the tortillas. Keep the cooked tortillas warm in a clean kitchen towel while you cook the remaining tortillas.

8. **Assemble the Tacos:**
- Fill each tortilla with a portion of the taco filling. Add your desired toppings such as shredded lettuce, diced tomatoes, shredded cheese, sliced avocado, sour cream, salsa, and fresh cilantro.

9. **Serving:**
- Serve the tacos immediately while the tortillas are warm.

10. **Storage:**
- Store any leftover tortillas in an airtight container at room temperature for up to 2 days. For longer storage, freeze the tortillas and reheat in a skillet before serving. Store any leftover taco filling in the refrigerator for up to 3 days.

BEEF BURGERS

Calories 450; Fat 25 g; Carb 30 g; Protein 25 g

SERVINGS:
8

PREP TIME: 30 minutes | **RISING TIME:** 4-6 hours | **COOKING TIME:** 15-20 minutes

---

UTENSILS:

- Large mixing bowl
- Measuring cups and spoons
- Kitchen scale
- Clean kitchen towel or plastic wrap
- Baking sheet
- Parchment paper or silicone baking mat
- Skillet or grill
- Spatula

INGREDIENTS:

Burger Buns:
- 1 cup (8 oz) sourdough discard
- 3 cups (13.5 oz) bread flour
- 1 cup (8 oz) warm water
- 2 tablespoons olive oil
- 2 tablespoons granulated sugar
- 2 teaspoons salt
- 1 teaspoon instant yeast (optional, for a quicker rise)
- 1 egg (for egg wash)
- Sesame seeds (optional, for topping)

Burger Patties:
- 1 pound ground beef (80% lean)
- 1 small onion, finely chopped
- 1 clove garlic, minced
- 1 teaspoon salt
- 1/2 teaspoon black pepper
- 1 teaspoon Worcestershire sauce (optional)

Toppings:
- Sliced cheese (cheddar, Swiss, or your favorite)
- Lettuce leaves
- Sliced tomatoes
- Sliced onions
- Pickles
- Ketchup, mustard, mayonnaise

INSTRUCTIONS:

1. **Prepare the Burger Bun Dough:**
- In a large mixing bowl, combine the sourdough discard, bread flour, warm water, olive oil, sugar, salt, and instant yeast (if using). Mix until a rough dough forms.

2. **Kneading:**
- Turn the dough out onto a lightly floured surface and knead for about 8-10 minutes until it becomes smooth and elastic. If the dough is too sticky, add a little more flour as needed.

3. **First Rise:**
- Place the dough back into the mixing bowl, cover it with a clean kitchen towel or plastic wrap, and let it rise at room temperature for 4-6 hours, or until it has doubled in size.

4. **Shaping the Buns:**
- Once the dough has risen, turn it out onto a lightly floured surface. Divide the dough into 8 equal pieces. Shape each piece into a ball and flatten it slightly to form a bun shape.

5. **Second Rise:**
- Place the shaped buns on a baking sheet lined with parchment paper or a silicone baking mat. Cover with a clean kitchen towel and let them rise for another 1-2 hours, or until they have puffed up.

6. **Preheat the Oven:**
- About 30 minutes before baking, preheat your oven to 375°F (190°C).

7. **Egg Wash:**
- In a small bowl, whisk together the egg with a tablespoon of water. Brush the tops of the buns with the egg wash and sprinkle with sesame seeds, if desired.

8. **Baking the Buns:**
- Bake in the preheated oven for 15-20 minutes, or until the buns are golden brown. Remove from the oven and let them cool on a wire rack.

9. **Prepare the Burger Patties:**
- In a mixing bowl, combine the ground beef, finely chopped onion, minced garlic, salt, black pepper, and Worcestershire sauce (if using). Mix until just combined. Divide the mixture into 4 equal portions and shape each into a patty.

10. **Cooking the Patties:**
- Heat a skillet or grill over medium-high heat. Cook the patties for about 4-5 minutes on each side, or until they reach your desired level of doneness. If using cheese, place a slice on each patty during the last minute of cooking to melt.

11. **Assembling the Burgers:**
- Slice the cooled burger buns in half. Place a cooked patty on the bottom half of each bun. Add your favorite toppings such as lettuce, sliced tomatoes, onions, pickles, ketchup, mustard, and mayonnaise. Top with the other half of the bun.

12. **Serving:**
- Serve the burgers while they are warm.

13. **Storage:**
- Store any leftover buns in an airtight container at room temperature for up to 2 days. For longer storage, freeze the buns and reheat in the oven before serving. Store any leftover cooked patties in the refrigerator for up to 3 days.

MEATLOAF

Calories 300; Fat 15 g; Carb 20 g; Protein 20 g

PREP TIME: 30 minutes	RISING TIME: 4-6 hours	BAKING TIME: 1 hours

UTENSILS:

- Large mixing bowl
- Measuring cups and spoons
- Kitchen scale
- Loaf pan (9x5 inch)
- Medium mixing bowl
- Whisk
- Rolling pin
- Baking sheet
- Parchment paper or silicone baking mat

INGREDIENTS:

Sourdough Dough:
- 1 cup (8 oz) sourdough discard
- 3 cups (13.5 oz) bread flour
- 1 cup (8 oz) warm water
- 2 tablespoons olive oil
- 2 teaspoons salt
- 1 teaspoon sugar
- 1 teaspoon instant yeast (optional, for a quicker rise)

Meatloaf:
- 1 pound ground beef (80% lean)
- 1 pound ground pork
- 1 small onion, finely chopped
- 2 cloves garlic, minced
- 1/2 cup grated Parmesan cheese
- 1/2 cup breadcrumbs
- 1/4 cup milk
- 2 large eggs
- 1/4 cup chopped fresh parsley (or 2 tablespoons dried parsley)
- 1 tablespoon Worcestershire sauce
- 1 teaspoon salt
- 1/2 teaspoon black pepper
- 1 teaspoon dried oregano
- 1 teaspoon dried thyme

Glaze:
- 1/2 cup ketchup
- 2 tablespoons brown sugar
- 1 tablespoon Dijon mustard

INSTRUCTIONS:

1. **Prepare the Sourdough Dough:**
- In a large mixing bowl, combine the sourdough discard, bread flour, warm water, olive oil, salt, sugar, and instant yeast (if using). Mix until a rough dough forms.
- Turn the dough out onto a lightly floured surface and knead for about 8-10 minutes until it becomes smooth and elastic. If the dough is too sticky, add a little more flour as needed.
- Place the dough back into the mixing bowl, cover it with a clean kitchen towel or plastic wrap, and let it rise at room temperature for 4-6 hours, or until it has doubled in size.

2. **Prepare the Meatloaf Mixture:**
- In a large mixing bowl, combine the ground beef, ground pork, finely chopped onion, minced garlic, grated Parmesan cheese, breadcrumbs, milk, eggs, chopped parsley, Worcestershire sauce, salt, black pepper, dried oregano, and dried thyme. Mix until all the ingredients are well incorporated. Be careful not to overmix, as this can make the meatloaf dense.

3. **Shape the Meatloaf:**
- Preheat your oven to 375°F (190°C). Lightly grease a loaf pan.
- Shape the meatloaf mixture into a loaf that will fit inside the loaf pan. Place the shaped meatloaf into the prepared loaf pan.

4. **Prepare the Glaze:**
- In a medium mixing bowl, whisk together the ketchup, brown sugar, and Dijon mustard until smooth.
- Spread half of the glaze evenly over the top of the meatloaf.

5. **Prebake the Meatloaf:**
- Bake the meatloaf in the preheated oven for 30 minutes to set it. Remove it from the oven and let it cool slightly.

6. **Prepare the Dough Wrap:**
- Roll out the sourdough dough on a lightly floured surface into a rectangle large enough to wrap around the meatloaf.
- Carefully remove the partially cooked meatloaf from the loaf pan and place it in the center of the rolled-out dough.
- Wrap the dough around the meatloaf, pinching the seams to seal. Place the wrapped meatloaf seam-side down on a baking sheet lined with parchment paper or a silicone baking mat.
- Brush the dough with a little olive oil.

7. **Final Baking:**
- Place the baking sheet with the wrapped meatloaf back into the oven and bake for an additional 30-35 minutes, or until the bread is golden brown and the internal temperature of the meatloaf reaches 160°F (70°C).

8. **Cooling:**
- Remove the meatloaf from the oven and let it rest for 10 minutes before slicing.

9. **Serving:**
- Slice the meatloaf and serve warm. It pairs well with mashed potatoes, steamed vegetables, or a side salad.

10. **Storage:**
- Store any leftover meatloaf in an airtight container in the refrigerator for up to 3 days. Reheat in the oven or microwave before serving.

SHEPHERD'S PIE

Calories 350; Fat 20 g; Carb 25 g; Protein 15 g

SERVINGS: 8

PREP TIME: 45 minutes　　**RISING TIME:** 4-6 hours　　**BAKING TIME:** 45-50 minutes

UTENSILS:

- Large mixing bowl
- Measuring cups and spoons
- Kitchen scale
- Large skillet
- Medium saucepan
- Baking dish (9x13 inch or equivalent)
- Rolling pin
- Pastry brush

INGREDIENTS:

Sourdough Dough:
- 1 cup (8 oz) sourdough discard
- 3 cups (13.5 oz) bread flour
- 1 cup (8 oz) warm water
- 2 tablespoons olive oil
- 2 teaspoons salt
- 1 teaspoon sugar
- 1 teaspoon instant yeast (optional, for a quicker rise)

Filling:
- 1 pound ground lamb or beef
- 1 small onion, finely chopped
- 2 cloves garlic, minced
- 1 cup carrots, diced
- 1 cup peas (fresh or frozen)
- 1 cup corn (fresh or frozen)
- 2 tablespoons tomato paste
- 1 cup beef or chicken broth
- 1 tablespoon Worcestershire sauce
- 1 teaspoon dried thyme
- 1 teaspoon dried rosemary
- 1/2 teaspoon salt
- 1/4 teaspoon black pepper
- 2 tablespoons all-purpose flour

Mashed Potato Topping:
- 2 cups (1 lb) mashed potatoes (prepared separately, see instructions)
- 1/2 cup grated Parmesan cheese
- 1/4 cup milk or cream
- 2 tablespoons unsalted butter
- 1 teaspoon salt
- 1/2 teaspoon black pepper

INSTRUCTIONS:

1. **Prepare the Sourdough Dough:**
- In a large mixing bowl, combine the sourdough discard, bread flour, warm water, olive oil, salt, sugar, and instant yeast (if using). Mix until a rough dough forms.
- Turn the dough out onto a lightly floured surface and knead for about 8-10 minutes until it becomes smooth and elastic. If the dough is too sticky, add a little more flour as needed.
- Place the dough back into the mixing bowl, cover it with a clean kitchen towel or plastic wrap, and let it rise at room temperature for 4-6 hours, or until it has doubled in size.

2. **Prepare the Mashed Potatoes:**
- Peel and dice 2 large potatoes. Place them in a medium saucepan and cover with water. Bring to a boil and cook until tender, about 15-20 minutes. Drain and return to the saucepan.
- Add the butter, milk or cream, salt, and pepper to the potatoes. Mash until smooth. Stir in the grated Parmesan cheese. Set aside.

3. **Prepare the Filling:**
- In a large skillet, cook the ground lamb or beef over medium heat until browned, breaking it up with a spoon as it cooks. Drain any excess fat.
- Add the chopped onion and minced garlic to the skillet. Cook until softened, about 5 minutes.
- Stir in the diced carrots, peas, and corn. Cook for another 5 minutes.
- Add the tomato paste, Worcestershire sauce, dried thyme, dried rosemary, salt, and black pepper. Stir to combine.
- Sprinkle the flour over the mixture and stir until evenly coated.
- Pour in the beef or chicken broth and bring to a simmer. Cook until the mixture thickens, about 5 minutes. Remove from heat and let it cool slightly.

4. **Preheat the Oven:**
- Preheat your oven to 375°F (190°C).

5. **Assemble the Shepherd's Pie:**
- Roll out the risen sourdough dough on a lightly floured surface into a rectangle large enough to fit your baking dish. Place the rolled-out dough into the baking dish, pressing it down and up the sides to form a crust.
- Pour the filling into the dough-lined baking dish, spreading it out evenly.
- Spoon the mashed potatoes over the filling and spread them out evenly. Use a fork to create a decorative pattern on the potatoes if desired.

6. **Baking:**
- Place the baking dish in the preheated oven and bake for 45-50 minutes, or until the dough is golden brown and the filling is bubbly.

7. **Cooling:**
- Remove the Shepherd's Pie from the oven and let it rest for 10 minutes before slicing and serving.

8. **Serving:**
- Serve the Shepherd's Pie warm. It pairs well with a side salad or steamed vegetables.

9. **Storage:**
- Store any leftover Shepherd's Pie in an airtight container in the refrigerator for up to 3 days. Reheat in the oven or microwave before serving.

QUESADILLAS

Calories 350; Fat 20 g; Carb 25 g; Protein 15 g

SERVINGS:
8

PREP TIME: 20 minutes   **TIME FOR THE REST:** 30 minutes   **COOKING TIME:** 10-15 minutes

---

UTENSILS:

- Large mixing bowl
- Measuring cups and spoons
- Kitchen scale
- Rolling pin
- Cast iron skillet or griddle
- Clean kitchen towel
- Spatula

INGREDIENTS:

Tortillas:
- 1 cup (8 oz) sourdough discard
- 2 cups (9 oz) all-purpose flour
- 1/2 teaspoon salt
- 2 tablespoons olive oil
- 1/2 cup (4 oz) warm water

Filling:
- 2 cups shredded cheese (cheddar, Monterey Jack, or your favorite blend)
- Optional: cooked chicken, beef, or vegetables (bell peppers, onions, spinach, etc.)

Toppings:
- Sour cream
- Salsa
- Guacamole
- Chopped fresh cilantro

INSTRUCTIONS:

1. **Prepare the Tortilla Dough:**
- In a large mixing bowl, combine the sourdough discard, flour, and salt. Add the olive oil and warm water. Mix until a dough forms.

2. **Kneading:**
- Turn the dough out onto a lightly floured surface and knead for about 5 minutes until smooth and elastic. If the dough is too sticky, add a little more flour as needed.

3. **Resting:**
- Place the dough back in the mixing bowl, cover it with a clean kitchen towel, and let it rest for 30 minutes. This allows the gluten to relax and makes the dough easier to roll out.

4. **Preheat the Skillet or Griddle:**
- Heat a cast iron skillet or griddle over medium-high heat.

5. **Shaping the Tortillas:**
- Divide the dough into 8 equal pieces. On a lightly floured surface, roll each piece into a thin circle, about 6-8 inches in diameter.

6. **Cooking the Tortillas:**
- Place each rolled-out dough circle onto the preheated skillet or griddle. Cook for about 1-2 minutes on each side, or until the tortilla is puffed and golden brown spots appear. Use tongs to flip the tortillas. Keep the cooked tortillas warm in a clean kitchen towel while you cook the remaining tortillas.

7. **Assembling the Quesadillas:**
- Place a tortilla on the skillet or griddle over medium heat. Sprinkle a generous amount of shredded cheese over half of the tortilla. Add any optional fillings (cooked chicken, beef, or vegetables) on top of the cheese.
- Fold the tortilla in half to cover the filling. Press down gently with a spatula.

8. **Cooking the Quesadillas:**
- Cook the quesadilla for about 2-3 minutes on each side, or until the cheese is melted and the tortilla is golden brown and crispy. Repeat with the remaining tortillas and fillings.

9. **Serving:**
- Cut the quesadillas into wedges and serve warm with sour cream, salsa, guacamole, and chopped fresh cilantro.

10. **Storage:**
- Store any leftover quesadillas in an airtight container in the refrigerator for up to 2 days. Reheat in the skillet or microwave before serving.

ENCHILADAS

Calories 300; Fat 15 g; Carb 25 g; Protein 15 g

SERVINGS:
12

PREP TIME: 30 minutes

COOKING TIME: 30 minutes

UTENSILS:

- Large mixing bowl
- Measuring cups and spoons
- Kitchen scale
- Rolling pin
- Cast iron skillet or griddle
- Medium saucepan
- 9x13 inch baking dish
- Aluminum foil

INGREDIENTS:

Tortillas:
- 1 cup (8 oz) sourdough discard
- 2 cups (9 oz) all-purpose flour
- 1/2 teaspoon salt
- 2 tablespoons olive oil
- 1/2 cup (4 oz) warm water

Enchilada Filling:
- 2 cups cooked and shredded chicken (or beef, or beans for a vegetarian option)
- 1 cup shredded cheese (cheddar, Monterey Jack, or your favorite blend)
- 1 cup cooked black beans or corn (optional)
- 1 small onion, finely chopped
- 1 small bell pepper, diced
- 2 cloves garlic, minced
- 1 tablespoon olive oil
- 1 teaspoon ground cumin
- 1 teaspoon chili powder
- Salt and pepper to taste

Enchilada Sauce:
- 2 tablespoons olive oil
- 2 tablespoons all-purpose flour
- 1/4 cup chili powder
- 1/2 teaspoon garlic powder
- 1/2 teaspoon dried oregano
- 1/2 teaspoon ground cumin
- 2 cups chicken or vegetable broth
- 1/2 teaspoon salt
- 1/4 teaspoon black pepper

Toppings:
- Extra shredded cheese
- Chopped fresh cilantro
- Sliced jalapeños (optional)
- Sour cream, Salsa

INSTRUCTIONS:

1. **Prepare the Tortilla Dough:**
- In a large mixing bowl, combine the sourdough discard, flour, and salt. Add the olive oil and warm water. Mix until a dough forms.

2. **Kneading:**
- Turn the dough out onto a lightly floured surface and knead for about 5 minutes until smooth and elastic. If the dough is too sticky, add a little more flour as needed.

3. **Resting:**
- Place the dough back in the mixing bowl, cover it with a clean kitchen towel, and let it rest for 30 minutes. This allows the gluten to relax and makes the dough easier to roll out.

4. **Prepare the Enchilada Sauce:**
- In a medium saucepan, heat the olive oil over medium heat. Stir in the flour and chili powder, and cook for about 1 minute.
- Add the garlic powder, dried oregano, ground cumin, broth, salt, and black pepper. Bring to a simmer, stirring constantly, and cook for about 10 minutes until the sauce thickens. Remove from heat and set aside.

5. **Prepare the Filling:**
- In a large skillet, heat the olive oil over medium heat. Add the chopped onion and bell pepper, and cook until softened, about 5 minutes.
- Add the minced garlic, ground cumin, and chili powder, and cook for another minute.
- Stir in the cooked chicken, shredded cheese, cooked black beans or corn (if using), and season with salt and pepper. Remove from heat and set aside.

6. **Preheat the Oven:**
- Preheat your oven to 375°F (190°C).

7. **Shaping the Tortillas:**
- Divide the dough into 10-12 equal pieces. On a lightly floured surface, roll each piece into a thin circle, about 6-8 inches in diameter.

8. **Cooking the Tortillas:**
- Heat a cast iron skillet or griddle over medium-high heat. Cook each rolled-out dough circle for about 1-2 minutes on each side, or until the tortilla is puffed and golden brown spots appear. Use tongs to flip the tortillas. Keep the cooked tortillas warm in a clean kitchen towel while you cook the remaining tortillas.

9. **Assembling the Enchiladas:**
- Spread a thin layer of the enchilada sauce on the bottom of a 9x13 inch baking dish.
- Place a portion of the filling in the center of each tortilla, roll it up, and place it seam-side down in the baking dish.
- Pour the remaining enchilada sauce over the rolled tortillas, and sprinkle with extra shredded cheese.

10. **Baking:**
- Cover the baking dish with aluminum foil and bake in the preheated oven for 20 minutes. Remove the foil and bake for an additional 10 minutes, or until the cheese is bubbly and golden brown.

11. **Serving:**
- Let the enchiladas cool for a few minutes before serving. Garnish with chopped fresh cilantro, sliced jalapeños, sour cream, and salsa.

12. **Storage:**
- Store any leftover enchiladas in an airtight container in the refrigerator for up to 3 days. Reheat in the oven or microwave before serving.

DESSERTS

BROWNIES

Calories 180; Fat 8 g; Carb 25 g; Protein 3 g

SERVINGS: 16

PREP TIME: 20 minutes

BAKING TIME: 25-30 minutes

UTENSILS:

- Large mixing bowl
- Medium mixing bowl
- Measuring cups and spoons
- Kitchen scale
- Whisk
- 9x9 inch baking pan
- Parchment paper

INGREDIENTS:

- 1 cup (8 oz) sourdough discard
- 1/2 cup (4 oz) unsalted butter, melted
- 1 cup (7 oz) granulated sugar
- 1/2 cup (3.5 oz) brown sugar
- 3 large eggs
- 1 teaspoon vanilla extract
- 3/4 cup (2.25 oz) unsweetened cocoa powder
- 1/2 teaspoon baking powder
- 1/2 teaspoon salt
- 1/2 cup (2.25 oz) all-purpose flour
- 1 cup (6 oz) chocolate chips or chunks (optional)
- 1/2 cup (2 oz) chopped nuts (optional)

INSTRUCTIONS:

1. **Preheat the Oven:**
- Preheat your oven to 350°F (175°C). Cover the inside of a baking pan measuring 9x9 inches with parchment paper, leaving some overhang for easy removal.
2. **Prepare the Wet Ingredients:**
- In a large mixing bowl, whisk together the melted butter, granulated sugar, and brown sugar until well combined.
- Add the eggs, one at a time, whisking well after each addition.
- Stir in the vanilla extract and sourdough discard until fully incorporated.
3. **Combine the Dry Ingredients:**
- In a medium mixing bowl, whisk together the cocoa powder, baking powder, salt, and all-purpose flour.
4. **Mix the Batter:**
- Gradually add the dry ingredients to the wet ingredients, mixing until just combined. Do not overmix.
- Fold in the chocolate chips or chunks and chopped nuts, if using.
5. **Bake the Brownies:**
- Pour the batter into the prepared baking pan, spreading it out evenly.
- Bake in the preheated oven for 25-30 minutes, or until a toothpick inserted into the center comes out with a few moist crumbs. The edges should be set, but the center should still be slightly soft.
6. **Cooling:**
- Remove the brownies from the oven and let them cool completely in the pan on a wire rack.
7. **Serving:**
- Once cooled, use the parchment paper overhang to lift the brownies out of the pan. Cut into squares and serve.
8. **Storage:**
- Store any leftover brownies in an airtight container at room temperature for up to 3 days. For longer storage, refrigerate for up to a week or freeze for up to 3 months.

SOURDOUGH COOKIES

Calories 120; Fat 6 g; Carb 16 g; Protein 2 g

SERVINGS: 24

PREP TIME: 15 minutes	CHILLING TIME: 1 hour	BAKING TIME: 12-15 minutes

UTENSILS:

- Large mixing bowl
- Medium mixing bowl
- Measuring cups and spoons
- Kitchen scale
- Whisk
- Baking sheet
- Parchment paper or silicone baking mat

INGREDIENTS:

- 1 cup (8 oz) sourdough discard
- 1/2 cup (4 oz) unsalted butter, softened
- 1/2 cup (3.5 oz) granulated sugar
- 1/2 cup (3.75 oz) brown sugar
- 1 large egg
- 1 teaspoon vanilla extract
- 1 1/2 cups (6.75 oz) all-purpose flour
- 1/2 teaspoon baking soda
- 1/2 teaspoon salt
- 1 cup (6 oz) chocolate chips or chunks
- 1/2 cup (2 oz) chopped nuts (optional)

INSTRUCTIONS:

1. **Prepare the Wet Ingredients:**
- In a large mixing bowl, cream together the softened butter, granulated sugar, and brown sugar until light and fluffy.
- Add the egg and vanilla extract, and mix until well combined.
- Stir in the sourdough discard until fully incorporated.
2. **Combine the Dry Ingredients:**
- In a medium mixing bowl, whisk together the flour, baking soda, and salt.
3. **Mix the Dough:**
- Gradually add the dry ingredients to the wet ingredients, mixing until just combined. Do not overmix.
- Fold in the chocolate chips or chunks and chopped nuts, if using.
4. **Chill the Dough:**
- Cover the dough with plastic wrap and refrigerate for at least 1 hour. Chilling the dough helps the cookies hold their shape and enhances the flavor.
5. **Preheat the Oven:**
- Preheat your oven to 350°F (175°C). Line a baking sheet with parchment or a silicone baking mat.
6. **Shape the Cookies:**
- Use a cookie scoop or spoon to drop rounded tablespoons of dough onto the prepared baking sheet, spacing them about 2 inches apart.
7. **Bake the Cookies:**
- Bake in the preheated oven for 12-15 minutes, or until the edges are golden brown and the centers are set.
- Remove from the oven and let the cookies cool on the baking sheet for 5 minutes before transferring them to a wire rack to cool completely.
8. **Serving:**
- Serve the cookies warm or at room temperature.
9. **Storage:**
- Store any leftover cookies in an airtight container at room temperature for up to 3 days. For longer storage, freeze the cookies for up to 3 months.

LEMON BARS

Calories 150; Fat 7 g; Carb 22 g; Protein 2 g

PREP TIME: 20 minutes   **COOKING TIME:** 3 hours   **BAKING TIME:** 50-60 minutes

---

UTENSILS:

- Large mixing bowl
- Medium mixing bowl
- Measuring cups and spoons
- Kitchen scale
- Whisk
- 9x13 inch glass baking dish
- Parchment paper
- Aluminum foil

INGREDIENTS:

For the Crust:
- 3/4 cup (1 1/2 sticks, 170g) unsalted butter, melted
- 1/2 cup (140g) sourdough discard
- 1 1/2 cups (210g) all-purpose flour
- 1/3 cup (50g) powdered sugar

For the Lemon Filling:
- 6 large eggs, beaten
- 3 cups (700g) granulated sugar
- 1/2 cup (70g) all-purpose flour
- 8 tablespoons (90g) fresh lemon juice

INSTRUCTIONS:

1. **Preheat the Oven:**
- Preheat your oven to 350°F (175°C). Cover the interior of a 9x13 inch glass baking dish with parchment paper, leaving enough overhang on the sides for easy removal.

2. **Prepare the Crust:**
- In a medium mixing bowl, combine the melted butter and sourdough discard. Whisk until well combined. Set aside.
- In a separate bowl, whisk together the all-purpose flour and powdered sugar.
- Add the wet ingredients to the flour mixture and mix until it resembles pie dough.
- Pour the dough into the prepared baking dish and gently press it with your hands to form an even layer.
- Bake for 25-30 minutes, or until the crust is lightly golden brown.

3. **Prepare the Lemon Filling:**
- While the crust is baking, prepare the lemon filling. In a large mixing bowl, beat the eggs with an electric mixer or whisk.
- Mix in the granulated sugar until well combined.
- Add the all-purpose flour and fresh lemon juice, and mix by hand until well-blended.

4. **Combine and Bake:**
- Once the crust is baked, remove the pan from the oven. Poke the shortbread with the prongs of a fork all around its surface to help the lemon custard adhere.
- Pour the lemon filling over the crust layer and return to the oven.
- Continue to bake for another 25-30 minutes, or until the lemon filling has set and no longer jiggles.

5. **Cooling:**
- Remove the lemon bars from the oven and place them on a wire rack to cool for at least an hour.
- Transfer to the refrigerator and chill for at least two hours to set.

6. **Serving:**
- Before serving, dust with powdered sugar if desired.
- Use the parchment paper overhang to lift the bars out of the baking dish and cut into squares or rectangles.

7. **Storage:**
- Store any leftover lemon bars in an airtight container in the refrigerator for up to 4 days. For longer storage, freeze the bars for up to 3 months.

SUMMER PIES

Calories 220; Fat 15 g; Carb 35 g; Protein 3 g

SERVINGS:
8

| PREP TIME: 30 minutes | CHILLING TIME: 1 hour | BAKING TIME: 45-60 minutes |

UTENSILS:

- Large mixing bowl
- Measuring cups and spoons
- Kitchen scale
- Rolling pin
- Pie dish (9-inch)
- Parchment paper
- Plastic wrap
- Pastry brush
- Aluminum foil or pie crust shield

INGREDIENTS:

For the Sourdough Pie Crust:
- 1 cup (2 sticks, 8 oz) unsalted butter, cold and cubed
- 2 1/2 cups (11.25 oz) all-purpose flour
- 1/2 teaspoon (0.1 oz) salt
- 1/2 cup (4 oz) sourdough discard
- 2-4 tablespoons (1-2 oz) ice water

For the Pie Filling:
- Your choice of filling (apple, cherry, pumpkin, etc.)

INSTRUCTIONS:

1. **Prepare the Sourdough Pie Crust:**
- In a large mixing bowl, combine the flour and salt.
- Add the cold, cubed butter to the flour mixture. Use a pastry cutter or your fingers to cut the butter into the flour until the mixture resembles coarse crumbs.
- Add the sourdough discard and mix until combined.
- Gradually add the ice water, one tablespoon at a time, mixing just until the dough comes together. Be careful not to overmix.
- Divide the dough in half, shape each half into a disk, wrap in plastic wrap, and refrigerate for at least 1 hour.
2. **Prepare the Pie Filling:**
- While the dough is chilling, prepare your chosen pie filling according to your recipe.
3. **Preheat the Oven:**
- Preheat your oven to 375°F (190°C).
4. **Roll Out the Dough:**
- On a lightly floured surface, roll out one disk of dough to fit your 9-inch pie dish. Place the rolled dough into the pie dish, pressing it gently to fit.
- Roll out the second disk of dough for the top crust or prepare it for a lattice topping.
5. **Assemble the Pie:**
- Pour the prepared filling into the pie crust.
- Cover with the top crust or lattice. Trim any excess dough and crimp the edges to seal.
- If using a solid top crust, cut a few slits in the top to allow steam to escape.
- Brush the top crust with a beaten egg or milk for a golden finish.
6. **Bake the Pie:**
- Cover the edges of the pie with aluminum foil or a pie crust shield to prevent over-browning.
- Bake in the preheated oven for 45-60 minutes, or until the crust is golden brown and the filling is bubbly.
- Remove the foil or pie crust shield during the last 15 minutes of baking to allow the edges to brown.
7. **Cooling:**
- Remove the pie from the oven and let it cool on a wire rack for at least 2 hours before serving to allow the filling to set.
8. **Serving:**
- Serve the pie warm or at room temperature with a scoop of ice cream or a dollop of whipped cream if desired.
9. **Storage:**
- Store any leftover pie in an airtight container in the refrigerator for up to 3 days. The pie can also be frozen for longer storage.

FRUIT COBBLER

Calories 220; Fat 9 g; Carb 34 g; Protein 2 g

PREP TIME: 15 minutes   **BAKING TIME: 45-50 minutes**

UTENSILS:

- Large mixing bowl
- Medium mixing bowl
- Measuring cups and spoons
- Kitchen scale
- Whisk
- 9x13 inch baking dish
- Medium saucepan
- Pastry brush

INGREDIENTS:

For the Sourdough Biscuit Topping:
- 1 cup (8 oz) sourdough discard
- 2 cups (9 oz) gluten-free all-purpose flour blend
- 1/4 cup (2 oz) granulated sugar
- 1 tablespoon (0.5 oz) baking powder
- 1/2 teaspoon (0.1 oz) salt
- 1/2 cup (1 stick, 4 oz) unsalted butter, cold and cubed
- 1/2 cup (4 oz) milk or buttermilk

For the Fruit Filling:
- 6 cups (about 30 oz) fresh or frozen fruit (peaches, berries, apples, etc.)
- 1 cup (7 oz) granulated sugar
- 1/4 cup (2 oz) brown sugar
- 2 tablespoons (1 oz) cornstarch
- 1 tablespoon (0.5 oz) lemon juice
- 1 teaspoon (0.1 oz) vanilla extract
- 1/2 teaspoon (0.1 oz) ground cinnamon (optional)

INSTRUCTIONS:

1. **Preheat the Oven:**
- Preheat your oven to 375°F (190°C). Grease a 9x13 inch baking dish and set aside.
2. **Prepare the Fruit Filling:**
- In a medium saucepan, combine the fresh or frozen fruit, granulated sugar, brown sugar, cornstarch, lemon juice, vanilla extract, and ground cinnamon (if using).
- Cook over medium heat, stirring frequently, until the mixture thickens and the fruit begins to break down. Pour the fruit filling into the prepared baking dish.
3. **Prepare the Sourdough Biscuit Topping:**
- In a large mixing bowl, whisk together the gluten-free all-purpose flour blend, granulated sugar, baking powder, and salt.
- Add the cold, cubed butter to the flour mixture. Use a pastry cutter or your fingers to cut the butter into the flour until the mixture resembles coarse crumbs.
- Stir in the sourdough discard and milk or buttermilk until just combined.
4. **Assemble the Cobbler:**
- Drop spoonfuls of the biscuit dough over the fruit filling in the baking dish. Spread the dough slightly to cover most of the fruit.
5. **Baking the Cobbler:**
- Bake in the preheated oven until the biscuit topping is golden brown and the fruit filling is bubbly.
6. **Cooling:**
- Remove the cobbler from the oven and let it cool on a wire rack for at least 15 minutes before serving.
7. **Serving:**
- Serve the cobbler warm with a scoop of ice cream or a dollop of whipped cream if desired.
8. **Storage:**
- Store any leftover cobbler in an airtight container in the refrigerator. Reheat in the oven or microwave before serving.

EASY CAKE

Calories 220; Fat 10 g; Carb 30 g; Protein 3 g

SERVINGS: 14

PREP TIME: 20 minutes

BAKING TIME: 30-35 minutes

UTENSILS:

- Large mixing bowl
- Medium mixing bowl
- Measuring cups and spoons
- Kitchen scale
- Whisk
- 9x13 inch baking pan or two 9-inch round cake pans
- Parchment paper

INGREDIENTS:

- 1 cup (8 oz) sourdough discard
- 2 cups (16 oz) granulated sugar
- 1 cup (8 oz) vegetable oil
- 3 large eggs
- 2 teaspoons vanilla extract
- 2 1/2 cups (11.25 oz) all-purpose flour
- 1 1/2 teaspoons baking powder
- 1 teaspoon baking soda
- 1/2 teaspoon salt
- 1 cup (8 oz) buttermilk or milk

Optional Add-ins:
- 1 cup (6 oz) chocolate chips or chopped nuts
- 1 cup (8 oz) shredded coconut
- 1 cup (8 oz) chopped fruit (e.g., apples, bananas, or berries)

INSTRUCTIONS:

1. **Preheat the Oven:**
- Preheat your oven to 350°F (175°C). Grease and flour a 9x13 inch baking pan or two 9-inch round cake pans. Line the bottoms with parchment paper for easier removal.
2. **Prepare the Wet Ingredients:**
- In a large mixing bowl, whisk together the sourdough discard, and vegetable oil until well combined.
- Add the eggs, one at a time, whisking well after each addition.
- Stir in the vanilla extract until fully incorporated.
3. **Combine the Dry Ingredients:**
- In a medium mixing bowl, whisk together the all-purpose flour, granulated sugar, baking powder, baking soda, and salt.
4. **Mix the Batter:**
- Gradually add the dry ingredients to the wet ingredients, alternating with the buttermilk or milk. Begin and end with the dry ingredients, mixing until just combined.
- If using any optional add-ins, gently fold them into the batter at this stage.
5. **Pour and Bake:**
- Pour the batter into the prepared baking pan(s), spreading it out evenly.
- Bake in the preheated oven for 30-35 minutes, or until a toothpick inserted into the center comes out clean. If using two round cake pans, check for doneness after 25-30 minutes.
6. **Cooling:**
- Remove the cake from the oven and let it cool in the pan(s) on a wire rack for 10 minutes.
- If using round cake pans, carefully run a knife around the edges and invert the cakes onto the wire rack. Remove the parchment paper and let the cakes cool completely.
7. **Serving:**
- Frost the cake with your favorite frosting or serve it plain. Top with fresh fruit or a dusting of powdered sugar if desired.
8. **Storage:**
- Store any leftover cake in an airtight container at room temperature. The cake can also be refrigerated or frozen for longer storage.

CUPCAKES

Calories 150; Fat 7 g; Carb 20 g; Protein 2 g

SERVINGS:
24

PREP TIME: 20 minutes   BAKING TIME: 18-22 minutes

UTENSILS:

- Large mixing bowl
- Medium mixing bowl
- Measuring cups and spoons
- Kitchen scale
- Whisk
- Muffin tin
- Paper muffin liners or non-stick cooking spray
- Ice cream scoop or spoon

INGREDIENTS:

- 1 cup (8 oz) sourdough discard
- 1 1/2 cups (6.75 oz) all-purpose flour
- 1/2 cup (3.5 oz) granulated sugar
- 1/4 cup (2 oz) brown sugar, packed
- 2 teaspoons baking powder
- 1/2 teaspoon baking soda
- 1/2 teaspoon salt
- 1/2 cup (4 oz) milk (dairy or non-dairy)
- 1/4 cup (2 oz) vegetable oil or melted butter
- 2 large eggs
- 1 teaspoon vanilla extract
- 1 cup (6 oz) chocolate chips or chunks (optional)
- 1/2 cup (2 oz) chopped nuts (optional)

For the Frosting:
- 1 cup (2 sticks, 8 oz) unsalted butter, softened
- 4 cups (16 oz) powdered sugar
- 1/4 cup (2 oz) heavy cream or milk
- 2 teaspoons vanilla extract
- Pinch of salt

INSTRUCTIONS:

1. **Preheat the Oven:**
- Preheat your oven to 375°F (190°C). Line a muffin tin with paper liners or lightly grease with non-stick cooking spray.
2. **Prepare the Dry Ingredients:**
- In a large mixing bowl, whisk together the flour, granulated sugar, brown sugar, baking powder, baking soda, and salt.
3. **Combine the Wet Ingredients:**
- In a medium mixing bowl, whisk together the sourdough discard, milk, vegetable oil or melted butter, eggs, vanilla extract (liquid) until well combined.
4. **Mix the Batter:**
- Pour the wet ingredients into the dry ingredients and stir until just combined. Be careful not to overmix; a few lumps are okay.
- If using any add-ins, gently fold them into the batter at this stage.
5. **Fill the Muffin Tin:**
- Use an ice cream scoop or spoon to divide the batter evenly among the muffin cups, filling each about 2/3 full.
6. **Bake the Cupcakes:**
- Bake in the preheated oven for 18-22 minutes, or until a toothpick inserted into the center of a cupcake comes out clean.
- Remove the cupcakes from the oven and let them cool in the tin for 5 minutes. Then transfer them to a wire rack to cool completely.
7. **Prepare the Frosting:**
- In a large mixing bowl, beat the softened butter until creamy.
- Gradually add the powdered sugar, 1 cup at a time, beating well after each addition.
- Add the heavy cream or milk, vanilla extract, and a pinch of salt. Beat until the frosting is light and fluffy.
8. **Frost the Cupcakes:**
- Once the cupcakes are completely cool, frost them using a piping bag or a spatula.
- Decorate with sprinkles, fresh fruit, or other toppings as desired.
9. **Serving:**
- Serve the cupcakes immediately.
10. **Storage:**
- Store any leftover cupcakes in an airtight container at room temperature for up to 2 days. Refrigerate for up to 5 days or freeze for longer storage.

CAKE BLONDIES

Calories 200; Fat 10 g; Carb 25 g; Protein 2 g

SERVINGS:
14

PREP TIME: 15 minutes

BAKING TIME: 25-30 minutes

UTENSILS:

- Large mixing bowl
- Medium mixing bowl
- Measuring cups and spoons
- Kitchen scale
- Whisk
- 9x13 inch baking pan
- Parchment paper

INGREDIENTS:

- 1 cup (8 oz) sourdough discard
- 1/2 cup (4 oz) unsalted butter, melted and slightly cooled
- 1 1/2 cups (12 oz) brown sugar, packed
- 1/2 cup (3.5 oz) granulated sugar
- 3 large eggs
- 1 teaspoon vanilla extract
- 1/2 cup (1.5 oz) cocoa powder
- 1/2 cup (2.25 oz) gluten-free all-purpose flour blend
- 1/4 teaspoon baking powder
- 1/4 teaspoon salt
- 1 cup (6 oz) chocolate chips or chunks (optional)

INSTRUCTIONS:

1. **Preheat the Oven:**
- Preheat your oven to 350°F (175°C). Line a 9x13 inch baking pan with parchment, leaving an overhang on the sides for easy removal.
2. **Prepare the Wet Ingredients:**
- In a large mixing bowl, whisk together the melted butter until smooth.
- Add the eggs one at a time, whisking well after each addition.
- Stir in the vanilla extract and sourdough discard until fully incorporated.
3. **Combine the Dry Ingredients:**
- In a medium mixing bowl, whisk together the brown sugar, and granulated sugar, cocoa powder, gluten-free all-purpose flour blend, baking powder, and salt.
4. **Mix the Batter:**
- Gradually add the dry ingredients to the wet ingredients, mixing until just combined. Do not overmix.
- Fold in the chocolate chips or chunks if using.
5. **Bake the Blondies:**
- Pour the batter into the prepared baking pan and spread it out evenly.
- Bake in the preheated oven for 25-30 minutes, or until a toothpick inserted into the center comes out with a few moist crumbs but no wet batter.
6. **Cooling:**
- Remove the blondies from the oven and let them cool completely in the pan on a wire rack.
7. **Serving:**
- Once cool, use the overhang of the parchment paper to lift the blondies out of the pan. Cut into squares or rectangles and serve immediately.
8. **Storage:**
- Store any leftover blondies in an airtight container at room temperature for up to 3 days. For longer storage, refrigerate for up to a week or freeze for up to 3 months.

CHEESECAKE

Calories 350; Fat 25 g; Carb 25 g; Protein 6 g

SERVINGS: 12

PREP TIME: 30 minutes   BAKING TIME: 60-70 minutes   CHILLING TIME: 4 hours or overnight

UTENSILS:

- Food processor or blender
- Large mixing bowl
- Medium mixing bowl
- Measuring cups and spoons
- Kitchen scale
- Electric mixer
- 9-inch springform pan
- Parchment paper
- Aluminum foil
- Roasting pan

INGREDIENTS:

For the Crust:
- 1 1/2 cups (6 oz) graham cracker crumbs
- 1/4 cup (2 oz) granulated sugar
- 1/2 cup (4 oz) unsalted butter, melted
- 1/2 cup (4 oz) sourdough discard

For the Cheesecake Filling:
- 3 (8 oz each) packages cream cheese, softened
- 1 cup (8 oz) granulated sugar
- 1/2 cup (4 oz) sourdough discard
- 1/2 cup (4 oz) sour cream
- 4 large eggs
- 1 teaspoon vanilla extract
- 2 tablespoons (1 oz) all-purpose flour
- 1 tablespoon (0.5 oz) lemon juice (optional)

INSTRUCTIONS:

1. **Preheat the Oven:**
- Preheat your oven to 325°F (163°C). Grease a 9-inch springform pan and line the bottom with parchment paper.

2. **Prepare the Crust:**
- In a medium mixing bowl, combine the graham cracker crumbs, granulated sugar, melted butter, and sourdough discard. Mix until the crumbs are well coated and the mixture resembles wet sand.
- Press the mixture evenly into the bottom of the prepared springform pan. Use the back of a spoon or a flat-bottomed glass to press it down firmly.
- Bake the crust in the preheated oven for 10 minutes. Remove from the oven and let it cool while you prepare the filling.

3. **Prepare the Filling:**
- In a large mixing bowl, beat the softened cream cheese with an electric mixer on medium speed until smooth and creamy.
- Add the granulated sugar and mix well.
- Add the sourdough discard and sour cream, and mix until fully incorporated.
- Add the eggs one at a time, beating well after each addition.
- Stir in the vanilla extract, all-purpose flour, and lemon juice (if using). Mix until just combined.

4. **Assemble the Cheesecake:**
- Pour the cheesecake filling over the cooled crust and spread it out evenly.
- Tap the pan gently on the counter to release any air bubbles.

5. **Prepare the Water Bath:**
- Wrap the bottom and sides of the springform pan with aluminum foil to prevent water from seeping in.
- Place the springform pan in a larger roasting pan. Pour hot water into the roasting pan until it reaches about halfway up the sides of the springform pan.

6. **Bake the Cheesecake:**
- Bake the cheesecake in the preheated oven for 60-70 minutes, or until the center is set but still slightly jiggly.
- Turn off the oven and crack the oven door open. Let the cheesecake cool in the oven for 1 hour.

7. **Chill the Cheesecake:**
- Remove the cheesecake from the oven and from the water bath. Remove the aluminum foil.
- Run a knife around the edge of the cheesecake to loosen it from the pan.
- Let the cheesecake cool to room temperature, then refrigerate for at least 4 hours, or overnight, until fully set.

8. **Serving:**
- Remove the cheesecake from the springform pan. Transfer to a serving plate.
- Slice and serve chilled. Garnish with fresh fruit, whipped cream, or a drizzle of chocolate sauce if desired.

9. **Storage:**
- Store any leftover cheesecake in an airtight container in the refrigerator for up to 5 days. The cheesecake can also be frozen for up to 3 months. To freeze, wrap individual slices in plastic wrap and then in aluminum foil before placing them in a freezer-safe bag or container.

TIRAMISU

Calories 200; Fat 10 g; Carb 25 g; Protein 2 g

SERVINGS: 12

PREP TIME: 45 minutes   **BAKING TIME:** 10-12 minutes   **CHILLING TIME:** 4 hours or overnight

---

UTENSILS:

- Large mixing bowl
- Medium mixing bowl
- Measuring cups and spoons
- Kitchen scale
- Electric mixer
- 9x13 inch baking dish or trifle dish
- Small saucepan
- Whisk
- Spatula
- Fine mesh sieve

INGREDIENTS:

For the Ladyfingers:
- 1 cup (8 oz) gluten-free sourdough discard
- 3 large eggs, separated
- 1/2 cup (4 oz) granulated sugar, divided
- 1 teaspoon vanilla extract
- 1/2 cup (2.25 oz) gluten-free all-purpose flour
- 1/4 teaspoon salt

For the Coffee Soak:
- 1 1/2 cups (12 oz) strong brewed coffee, cooled
- 1/4 cup (2 oz) coffee liqueur (optional)

For the Mascarpone Filling:
- 1 cup (8 oz) heavy cream
- 1 cup (8 oz) mascarpone cheese, softened
- 1/2 cup (4 oz) granulated sugar
- 1 teaspoon vanilla extract
- 3 large egg yolks

For Dusting:
- 2 tablespoons (0.5oz) unsweetened cocoa powder

INSTRUCTIONS:

1. **Prepare the Ladyfingers:**
- Preheat your oven to 350°F (177°C). Line two baking sheets with parchment paper.
- In a large mixing bowl, beat the egg yolks and half of the granulated sugar until thick and pale. Stir in the vanilla extract and sourdough discard.
- In a separate bowl, sift together the flour and salt. Gradually fold the flour mixture into the egg yolk mixture until just combined.
- In a clean medium mixing bowl, beat the egg whites with an electric mixer until soft peaks form. Gradually add the remaining granulated sugar and continue to beat until stiff peaks form.
- Gently fold the beaten egg whites into the batter until no streaks remain.
- Transfer the batter to a piping bag fitted with a large round tip. Pipe 3-inch long ladyfingers onto the prepared baking sheets, spacing them about 1 inch apart.
- Bake in the preheated oven for 10-12 minutes, or until the ladyfingers are lightly golden and set. Let them cool on the baking sheets for a few minutes before transferring to a wire rack to cool completely.

2. **Prepare the Coffee Soak:**
- In a small saucepan, combine the brewed coffee and coffee liqueur (if using). Heat over low heat until just warm. Remove from heat and let it cool to room temperature.

3. **Prepare the Mascarpone Filling:**
- In a large mixing bowl, beat the heavy cream with an electric mixer until stiff peaks form. Set aside.
- In another bowl, beat the mascarpone cheese, granulated sugar, and vanilla extract until smooth and creamy.
- In a small saucepan, whisk the egg yolks over low heat until slightly thickened and pale. Be careful not to overcook the yolks. Remove from heat and let cool slightly.
- Gently fold the whipped cream into the mascarpone mixture, followed by the cooled egg yolks. Mix until well combined.

4. **Assemble the Tiramisu:**
- Quickly dip each ladyfinger into the coffee soak, ensuring they are well saturated but not soggy. Line the bottom of a 9x13 inch baking dish with a layer of soaked ladyfingers.
- Spread half of the mascarpone filling over the ladyfingers, smoothing it out with a spatula.
- Repeat with another layer of soaked ladyfingers and the remaining mascarpone filling.
- Cover and refrigerate for at least 4 hours, or overnight, to allow the flavors to meld and the tiramisu to set.

5. **Serving:**
- Before serving, dust the top of the tiramisu with unsweetened cocoa powder using a fine mesh sieve.
- Slice and serve chilled. Garnish with chocolate shavings or coffee beans if desired.

6. **Storage:**
- Store any leftover tiramisu in an airtight container in the refrigerator for up to 3 days. Tiramisu can also be frozen for longer storage; wrap individual slices in plastic wrap and then in aluminum foil before placing them in a freezer-safe bag or container.

GLUTEN-FREE OPTIONS

GLUTEN-FREE PANCAKES

Calories 160; Fat 6 g; Carb 22 g; Protein 4 g

SERVINGS:
12

PREP TIME: 10 minutes   **TIME FOR THE REST:** 30 minutes   **COOKING TIME:** 20 minutes

---

UTENSILS:

- Large mixing bowl
- Medium mixing bowl
- Measuring cups and spoons
- Kitchen scale
- Whisk
- Non-stick skillet or griddle
- Spatula

INGREDIENTS:

- 1 cup (8 oz) gluten-free sourdough discard
- 1 cup (8 oz) gluten-free all-purpose flour
- 1 tablespoon granulated sugar
- 1 teaspoon baking powder
- 1/2 teaspoon baking soda
- 1/2 teaspoon salt
- 1 cup (8 oz) milk (dairy or non-dairy)
- 2 large eggs
- 2 tablespoons melted butter or oil (dairy or non-dairy), plus more for cooking
- 1 teaspoon vanilla extract

INSTRUCTIONS:

1. **Prepare the Batter:**
- In a large mixing bowl, whisk together the gluten-free sourdough discard, gluten-free all-purpose flour, granulated sugar, baking powder, baking soda, and salt.
2. **Combine Wet Ingredients:**
- In a medium mixing bowl, whisk together the milk, eggs, melted butter or oil, and vanilla extract until well combined.
3. **Mix the Batter:**
- Pour the wet ingredients into the dry ingredients and stir until just combined. Be careful not to overmix; a few lumps are okay. Let the batter rest for 30 minutes to allow the gluten-free flour to hydrate.
4. **Preheat the Skillet or Griddle:**
- Heat a non-stick skillet or griddle over medium heat. Lightly grease with butter or oil.
5. **Cook the Pancakes:**
- Pour about 1/4 cup of batter onto the skillet for each pancake. Cook until bubbles form on the surface and the edges look set. Flip and cook for another 1-2 minutes, or until golden brown and cooked through.
- Adjust the heat as needed to prevent burning and ensure even cooking.
6. **Serving:**
- Serve the pancakes warm with your favorite toppings such as maple syrup, fresh fruit, or yogurt.
7. **Storage:**
- Store any leftover pancakes in an airtight container in the refrigerator for up to 3 days. Reheat in a toaster or skillet before serving. Pancakes can also be frozen for longer storage; place a piece of parchment paper between each pancake and store in a freezer-safe bag or container. Reheat from frozen in a toaster or skillet.

GLUTEN-FREE BREAD

Calories 120; Fat 2 g; Carb 22 g; Protein 3 g

SERVINGS:
8-10

PREP TIME: 15 minutes   **RISING TIME:** 4-6 hours   **BAKING TIME:** 50-60 minutes

UTENSILS:

- Large mixing bowl
- Measuring cups and spoons
- Kitchen scale
- Whisk
- 9x5 inch loaf pan
- Parchment paper
- Plastic wrap or clean kitchen towel

INGREDIENTS:

- 1 cup (8 oz) gluten-free sourdough discard
- 1 1/2 cups (12 oz) warm water
- 2 tablespoons olive oil
- 1 tablespoon honey or maple syrup
- 3 cups (13.5 oz) gluten-free all-purpose flour blend
- 1 cup (4 oz) gluten-free oat flour
- 1/4 cup (1 oz) psyllium husk powder
- 1 tablespoon baking powder
- 2 teaspoons salt
- 1 teaspoon apple cider vinegar

INSTRUCTIONS:

1. **Prepare the Dough:**
- In a large mixing bowl, whisk together the gluten-free sourdough discard, warm water, olive oil, and honey or maple syrup until well combined.
- Add the gluten-free all-purpose flour blend, gluten-free oat flour, psyllium husk powder, baking powder, and salt to the wet ingredients. Mix until a thick, sticky dough forms.
- Add the apple cider vinegar and mix until incorporated.
2. **First Rise:**
- Cover the mixing bowl with plastic wrap or a clean kitchen towel. Let the dough rise at room temperature for 4-6 hours, or until it has doubled in size.
3. **Prepare the Loaf Pan:**
- Line a 9x5 inch loaf pan with parchment paper, leaving some overhang on the sides for easy removal.
4. **Shape the Dough:**
- Transfer the risen dough to the prepared loaf pan, smoothing the top with a spatula. Cover the pan with plastic wrap or a clean kitchen towel and let it rise for another 30-45 minutes, or until the dough reaches the top of the pan.
5. **Preheat the Oven:**
- Preheat your oven to 375°F (190°C).
6. **Bake the Bread:**
- Bake the bread in the preheated oven for 50-60 minutes, or until the crust is golden brown and a toothpick inserted into the center comes out clean. If the crust starts to brown too quickly, tent the bread with aluminum foil.
7. **Cooling:**
- Remove the bread from the oven and let it cool in the pan for 10 minutes. Then, use the parchment paper overhang to lift the bread out of the pan and transfer it to a wire rack to cool completely before slicing.
8. **Serving:**
- Slice the bread and serve with your favorite spreads, soups, or salads.
9. **Storage:**
- Store any leftover bread in an airtight container at room temperature for up to 3 days. For longer storage, refrigerate for up to a week or freeze for up to 3 months. To freeze, slice the bread and wrap each slice in plastic wrap before placing them in a freezer-safe bag or container.

GLUTEN-FREE CRACKERS

Calories 140; Fat 6 g; Carb 20 g; Protein 2 g

SERVINGS: 4-6

PREP TIME: 15 minutes	TIME FOR THE REST: 1 hour	BAKING TIME: 20-25 minutes

UTENSILS:

- Large mixing bowl
- Measuring cups and spoons
- Kitchen scale
- Rolling pin
- Baking sheet
- Parchment paper
- Pizza cutter or sharp knife

INGREDIENTS:

- 1 cup (8 oz) gluten-free sourdough discard
- 1 cup (4.5 oz) gluten-free all-purpose flour blend
- 1/4 cup (2 oz) olive oil
- 1/2 teaspoon salt
- 1/2 teaspoon garlic powder (optional)
- 1/2 teaspoon dried herbs (such as rosemary, thyme, or oregano) (optional)
- Sea salt, for sprinkling

INSTRUCTIONS:

1. **Prepare the Dough:**
- In a large mixing bowl, combine the gluten-free sourdough discard, gluten-free all-purpose flour blend, olive oil, salt, garlic powder (if using), and dried herbs (if using). Mix until a smooth dough forms.
2. **Resting:**
- Cover the dough with plastic wrap or a clean kitchen towel and let it rest at room temperature for 1 hour. This allows the flavors to meld and the dough to become easier to work with.
3. **Preheat the Oven:**
- Preheat your oven to 350°F (175°C). Line a baking sheet with parchment paper.
4. **Roll Out the Dough:**
- Place the dough between two sheets of parchment paper. Use a rolling pin to roll the dough out to about 1/8-inch thickness. The thinner you roll the dough, the crispier the crackers will be.
5. **Cut the Crackers:**
- Remove the top sheet of parchment paper. Use a pizza cutter or sharp knife to cut the dough into squares or rectangles of your desired size. Carefully transfer the parchment paper with the cut dough onto the baking sheet.
6. **Add Toppings:**
- Sprinkle the dough lightly with sea salt or any other desired toppings (such as sesame seeds or poppy seeds).
7. **Bake the Crackers:**
- Bake in the preheated oven for 20-25 minutes, or until the crackers are golden brown and crispy. Rotate the baking sheet halfway through the baking time to ensure even baking.
8. **Cooling:**
- Remove the crackers from the oven and let them cool completely on the baking sheet. They will continue to crisp up as they cool.
9. **Serving:**
- Serve the crackers on their own or with your favorite dips, cheeses, or spreads.
10. **Storage:**
- Store any leftover crackers in an airtight container at room temperature for up to 1 week. If they lose their crispness, you can re-crisp them in the oven at 350°F (175°C) for a few minutes.

GLUTEN-FREE PIZZA CRUST

Calories 170; Fat 5 g; Carb 26 g; Protein 3 g

PREP TIME: 20 minutes	RISING TIME: 2-4 hours	BAKING TIME: 15-20 minutes

UTENSILS:

- Large mixing bowl
- Measuring cups and spoons
- Kitchen scale
- Whisk
- Baking sheet or pizza stone
- Parchment paper
- Rolling pin or your hands

INGREDIENTS:

- 1 cup (8oz) gluten-free sourdough discard
- 1 cup (4.5 oz) gluten-free all-purpose flour blend
- 1/2 cup (2 oz) gluten-free oat flour
- 1/4 cup (1 oz) tapioca starch
- 1 teaspoon salt
- 1 teaspoon baking powder
- 1 teaspoon dried oregano (optional)
- 1 teaspoon dried basil (optional)
- 1/2 cup (4 oz) warm water
- 2 tablespoons olive oil
- 1 teaspoon honey or maple syrup

INSTRUCTIONS:

1. **Prepare the Dough:**
- In a large mixing bowl, whisk together the gluten-free sourdough discard, gluten-free all-purpose flour blend, gluten-free oat flour, tapioca starch, salt, baking powder, dried oregano, and dried basil (if using).
- Add the warm water, olive oil, and honey or maple syrup to the dry ingredients. Mix until a sticky dough forms.
2. **First Rise:**
- Cover the mixing bowl with plastic wrap or a clean kitchen towel. Let the dough rise at room temperature for 2-4 hours, or until it has doubled in size.
3. **Preheat the Oven:**
- About 30 minutes before baking, preheat your oven to 450°F (230°C). If using a pizza stone, place it in the oven to preheat. If using a baking sheet, line it with parchment.
4. **Shape the Dough:**
- Transfer the risen dough to a piece of parchment paper. Use your hands or a rolling pin to shape the dough into a circle or rectangle about 1/4 inch thick. If the dough is too sticky, lightly flour your hands or the rolling pin with gluten-free flour.
5. **Parbake the Crust:**
- Transfer the dough (with the parchment paper) to the preheated pizza stone or baking sheet. Bake in the preheated oven for 10 minutes, or until the crust is set and slightly golden.
6. **Add Toppings:**
- Remove the parbaked crust from the oven. Add your favorite pizza toppings, such as sauce, cheese, vegetables, and meats.
7. **Bake the Pizza:**
- Return the pizza to the oven and bake for an additional 10-15 minutes, or until the toppings are cooked and the cheese is melted and bubbly.
8. **Serving:**
- Remove the pizza from the oven and let it cool for a few minutes before slicing and serving.
9. **Storage:**
- Store any leftover pizza in an airtight container in the refrigerator for up to 3 days. Reheat in the oven or microwave before serving. The parbaked crust can also be frozen for longer storage; wrap it tightly in plastic wrap and aluminum foil before freezing.

GLUTEN-FREE MUFFINS

Calories 180; Fat 7 g; Carb 24 g; Protein 3 g

SERVINGS:
12

PREP TIME: 15 minutes   **BAKING TIME:** 20-25 minutes

UTENSILS:

- Large mixing bowl
- Medium mixing bowl
- Measuring cups and spoons
- Kitchen scale
- Whisk
- Muffin tin
- Paper muffin liners or non-stick cooking spray

INGREDIENTS:

- 1 cup (8oz) gluten-free sourdough discard
- 1 1/2 cups (6.75 oz) gluten-free all-purpose flour blend
- 1/2 cup (3.5 oz) granulated sugar
- 1/4 cup (2 oz) brown sugar, packed
- 2 teaspoons baking powder
- 1/2 teaspoon baking soda
- 1/2 teaspoon salt
- 1/2 teaspoon ground cinnamon (optional)
- 1/2 cup (4 oz) milk (dairy or non-dairy)
- 1/4 cup (2 oz) vegetable oil or melted butter
- 2 large eggs
- 1 teaspoon vanilla extract
- 1 cup (6 oz) add-ins (such as chocolate chips, blueberries, or nuts) (optional)

INSTRUCTIONS:

1. **Preheat the Oven:**
- Preheat your oven to 375°F (191°C). Line a muffin tin with paper liners or lightly grease with non-stick cooking spray.
2. **Prepare the Dry Ingredients:**
- In a large mixing bowl, whisk together the gluten-free all-purpose flour blend, granulated sugar, brown sugar, baking powder, baking soda, salt, and ground cinnamon (if using).
3. **Combine the Wet Ingredients:**
- In a medium mixing bowl, whisk together the gluten-free sourdough discard, milk, vegetable oil or melted butter, eggs, and vanilla extract until well combined.
4. **Mix the Batter:**
- Pour the wet ingredients into the dry ingredients and stir until just combined. Be careful not to overmix; a few lumps are okay.
- If using any add-ins, gently fold them into the batter at this stage.
5. **Fill the Muffin Tin:**
- Use a spoon or a cookie scoop to divide the batter evenly among the muffin cups, filling each about 2/3 full.
6. **Bake the Muffins:**
- Bake in the preheated oven for 20-25 minutes, or until a toothpick inserted into the center of a muffin comes out clean.
- Remove the muffins from the oven and let them cool in the tin for 5 minutes. Then transfer them to a wire rack to cool completely.
7. **Serving:**
- Serve the muffins warm or at room temperature.
8. **Storage:**
- Store any leftover muffins in an airtight container at room temperature for up to 2 days. For longer storage, refrigerate for up to a week or freeze for up to 3 months. Reheat in the microwave or oven before serving.

GLUTEN-FREE COOKIES

Calories 130; Fat 6 g; Carb 18 g; Protein 2 g

SERVINGS: 24

PREP TIME: 15 minutes	CHILLING TIME: 1 hour	BAKING TIME: 12-15 minutes

UTENSILS:

- Large mixing bowl
- Medium mixing bowl
- Measuring cups and spoons
- Kitchen scale
- Whisk
- Baking sheet
- Parchment paper or silicone baking mat

INGREDIENTS:

- 1 cup (8oz) gluten-free sourdough discard
- 1/2 cup (4 oz) unsalted butter, softened
- 1/2 cup (3.5 oz) granulated sugar
- 1/2 cup (3.75 oz) brown sugar, packed
- 1 large egg
- 1 teaspoon vanilla extract
- 1 1/2 cups (6.75 oz) gluten-free all-purpose flour blend
- 1/2 teaspoon baking soda
- 1/2 teaspoon salt
- 1 cup (6 oz) chocolate chips or chunks
- 1/2 cup (2 oz) chopped nuts (optional)

INSTRUCTIONS:

1. **Prepare the Wet Ingredients:**
- In a large mixing bowl, cream together the softened butter, granulated sugar, and brown sugar until light and fluffy.
- Add the egg and vanilla extract, and mix until well combined.
- Stir in the gluten-free sourdough discard until fully incorporated.
2. **Combine the Dry Ingredients:**
- In a medium mixing bowl, whisk together the gluten-free all-purpose flour blend, baking soda, and salt.
3. **Mix the Dough:**
- Gradually add the dry ingredients to the wet ingredients, mixing until just combined. Do not overmix.
- Fold in the chocolate chips or chunks and chopped nuts, if using.
4. **Chill the Dough:**
- Cover the dough with plastic wrap and refrigerate for at least 1 hour. Chilling the dough helps the cookies hold their shape and enhances the flavor.
5. **Preheat the Oven:**
- Preheat your oven to 350°F (175°C). Line a baking sheet with parchment or a silicone baking mat.
6. **Shape the Cookies:**
- Use a cookie scoop or spoon to drop rounded tablespoons of dough onto the prepared baking sheet, spacing them about 2 inches apart.
7. **Bake the Cookies:**
- Bake in the preheated oven for 12-15 minutes, or until the edges are golden brown and the centers are set.
- Remove from the oven and let the cookies cool on the baking sheet for 5 minutes before transferring them to a wire rack to cool completely.
8. **Serving:**
- Serve the cookies warm or at room temperature.
9. **Storage:**
- Store any leftover cookies in an airtight container at room temperature for up to 3 days. For longer storage, freeze the cookies for up to 3 months.

GLUTEN-FREE BROWNIES

Calories 190; Fat 8 g; Carb 28 g; Protein 2 g

SERVINGS:
12-16

PREP TIME: 15 minutes   **BAKING TIME:** 25-30 minutes

UTENSILS:

- Large mixing bowl
- Medium mixing bowl
- Measuring cups and spoons
- Kitchen scale
- Whisk
- 9x13 inch baking pan
- Parchment paper

INGREDIENTS:

- 1 cup (8oz) gluten-free sourdough discard
- 1/2 cup (4 oz) unsalted butter, melted and slightly cooled
- 1 cup (7 oz) granulated sugar
- 1/2 cup (3.75 oz) brown sugar, packed
- 3 large eggs
- 1 teaspoon vanilla extract
- 1/2 cup (1.5 oz) cocoa powder
- 1/2 cup (2.25 oz) gluten-free all-purpose flour blend
- 1/4 teaspoon baking powder
- 1/4 teaspoon salt
- 1 cup (6 oz) chocolate chips or chunks (optional)

INSTRUCTIONS:

1. **Preheat the Oven:**
- Preheat your oven to 350°F (175°C). Line a 9x13 inch baking pan with parchment, leaving an overhang on the sides for easy removal.
2. **Prepare the Wet Ingredients:**
- In a large mixing bowl, whisk together the melted butter, granulated sugar, and brown sugar until smooth.
- Add the eggs one at a time, whisking well after each addition.
- Stir in the vanilla extract and gluten-free sourdough discard until fully incorporated.
3. **Combine the Dry Ingredients:**
- In a medium mixing bowl, whisk together the cocoa powder, gluten-free all-purpose flour blend, baking powder, and salt.
4. **Mix the Batter:**
- Gradually add the dry ingredients to the wet ingredients, mixing until just combined. Do not overmix.
- Fold in the chocolate chips or chunks if using.
5. **Bake the Brownies:**
- Pour the batter into the prepared baking pan and spread it out evenly.
- Bake in the preheated oven for 25-30 minutes, or until a toothpick inserted into the center comes out with a few moist crumbs but no wet batter.
6. **Cooling:**
- Remove the brownies from the oven and let them cool completely in the pan on a wire rack.
7. **Serving:**
- Once cooled, use the parchment paper overhang to lift the brownies out of the pan. Cut into squares or rectangles and serve.
8. **Storage:**
- Store any leftover brownies in an airtight container at room temperature for up to 3 days. For longer storage, refrigerate for up to a week or freeze for up to 3 months.

GLUTEN-FREE BANANA BREAD

Calories 200; Fat 8 g; Carb 30 g; Protein 2 g

SERVINGS: 10-12

PREP TIME: 15 minutes   **BAKING TIME:** 50-60 minutes

UTENSILS:

- Large mixing bowl
- Medium mixing bowl
- Measuring cups and spoons
- Kitchen scale
- Whisk
- 9x5 inch loaf pan
- Parchment paper

INGREDIENTS:

- 1 cup (8 oz) gluten-free sourdough discard
- 1 1/2 cups (6.75 oz) gluten-free all-purpose flour blend
- 1 teaspoon baking soda
- 1/2 teaspoon salt
- 1 teaspoon ground cinnamon
- 1/2 teaspoon ground nutmeg (optional)
- 1/2 cup (4 oz) unsalted butter, melted and cooled
- 1/2 cup (3.75 oz) brown sugar, packed
- 1/4 cup (2 oz) granulated sugar
- 2 large eggs
- 1 teaspoon vanilla extract
- 1 cup (8 oz) mashed ripe bananas (about 2 large bananas)
- 1/2 cup (4 oz) plain yogurt or sour cream (dairy or non-dairy)
- 1/2 cup (3 oz) chopped nuts or chocolate chips (optional)

INSTRUCTIONS:

1. **Preheat the Oven:**
- Preheat your oven to 350°F (175°C). Line a 9x5 inch loaf pan with parchment paper, leaving an overhang on the sides for easy removal.
2. **Prepare the Dry Ingredients:**
- In a medium mixing bowl, whisk together the gluten-free all-purpose flour blend, baking soda, salt, ground cinnamon, and ground nutmeg (if using).
3. **Prepare the Wet Ingredients:**
- In a large mixing bowl, whisk together the gluten-free sourdough discard, melted butter, brown sugar, and granulated sugar until well combined.
- Add the eggs and vanilla extract, and whisk until smooth.
- Stir in the mashed ripe bananas and plain yogurt or sour cream until well incorporated.
4. **Combine the Ingredients:**
- Gradually add the dry ingredients to the wet ingredients, mixing until just combined. Do not overmix.
- Fold in the chopped nuts or chocolate chips if using.
5. **Pour the Batter:**
- Pour the batter into the prepared loaf pan and spread it out evenly.
6. **Bake the Bread:**
- Bake in the preheated oven for 50-60 minutes, or until a toothpick inserted into the center comes out clean.
- If the bread starts to brown too quickly, cover it loosely with aluminum foil.
7. **Cooling:**
- Remove the banana bread from the oven and let it cool in the pan for 10 minutes.
- Use the parchment paper overhang to lift the bread out of the pan and transfer it to a wire rack to cool completely.
8. **Serving:**
- Slice and serve the banana bread at room temperature or slightly warm.
9. **Storage:**
- Store any leftover banana bread in an airtight container at room temperature for up to 3 days. For longer storage, refrigerate for up to a week or freeze for up to 3 months.

GLUTEN-FREE BAGELS

Calories 250; Fat 2 g; Carb 50 g; Protein 5 g

SERVINGS: 8

PREP TIME: 15 minutes **RISING TIME:** 4-6 hours **BOILING AND BAKING TIME:** 20-25 minutes

UTENSILS:

- Large mixing bowl
- Measuring cups and spoons
- Kitchen scale
- Whisk
- Parchment paper
- Baking sheet
- Large pot
- Slotted spoon
- Cooling rack
- Pastry brush

INGREDIENTS:

- 1 cup (8 oz) gluten-free sourdough discard
- 1 cup (8 oz) warm water
- 2 tablespoons honey or sugar
- 2 teaspoons instant yeast (optional, for a quicker rise)
- 3 cups (13.5 oz) gluten-free all-purpose flour blend
- 1/2 cup (2oz) gluten-free oat flour
- 1/4 cup (1oz) psyllium husk powder
- 1 1/2 teaspoons salt
- 1 tablespoon olive oil

For Boiling:
- 8 cups water
- 2 tablespoons honey or sugar

For Topping:
- Sesame seeds, poppy seeds, everything bagel seasoning, or other toppings of choice
- 1 egg, beaten (for egg wash)

INSTRUCTIONS:

1. **Prepare the Dough:**
- In a large mixing bowl, combine the gluten-free sourdough discard, warm water, honey or sugar, and instant yeast (if using). Mix until well combined.
- Add the gluten-free all-purpose flour blend, gluten-free oat flour, psyllium husk powder, and salt to the wet ingredients. Mix until a dough forms.
- Add the olive oil and knead the dough until smooth and elastic. If the dough is too sticky, add a little more flour as needed.

2. **First Rise:**
- Cover the mixing bowl with plastic wrap or a clean kitchen towel. Let the dough rise at room temperature for 4-6 hours, or until it has doubled in size.

3. **Shape the Bagels:**
- Once the dough has risen, turn it out onto a lightly floured surface. Divide the dough into 8 equal pieces.
- Shape each piece into a ball and then use your thumb to create a hole in the center of each ball, stretching it into a bagel shape. Place the shaped bagels on a baking sheet lined with parchment paper.

4. **Second Rise:**
- Cover the baking sheet with a clean kitchen towel and let the bagels rise for another 30-45 minutes, or until they have puffed up.

5. **Boil the Bagels:**
- In a large pot, bring the water and honey or sugar to a boil.
- Carefully lower a few bagels at a time into the boiling water using a slotted spoon. Boil each bagel for 1-2 minutes on each side. Remove the boiled bagels and place them back on the baking sheet.

6. **Preheat the Oven:**
- Preheat your oven to 425°F (220°C).

7. **Add Toppings:**
- Brush the boiled bagels with the beaten egg to create a shiny crust.
- Sprinkle with sesame seeds, poppy seeds, everything bagel seasoning, or other toppings of choice.

8. **Bake the Bagels:**
- Bake in the preheated oven for 20-25 minutes, or until the bagels are golden brown and cooked through.

9. **Cooling:**
- Remove the bagels from the oven and let them cool on a wire rack.

10. **Serving:**
- Serve the bagels warm or at room temperature. They can be enjoyed plain, toasted, or with your favorite spreads and toppings.

11. **Storage:**
- Store any leftover bagels in an airtight container at room temperature for up to 2 days. For longer storage, refrigerate for up to a week or freeze for up to 3 months. Reheat in the oven or toaster before serving.

GLUTEN-FREE DONUTS

Calories 220; Fat 10 g; Carb 30 g; Protein 2 g

PREP TIME: 30 minutes   **RISING TIME: 4-6 hours**   **FRYING TIME: 15-20 minutes**

UTENSILS:

- Large mixing bowl
- Measuring cups and spoons
- Kitchen scale
- Whisk
- Rolling pin
- Donut cutter or round cookie cutters
- Baking sheet
- Parchment paper
- Large pot or deep fryer
- Slotted spoon
- Cooling rack

INGREDIENTS:

- 1 cup (8oz) gluten-free sourdough discard
- 1 cup (8 oz) warm milk (dairy or non-dairy)
- 1/4 cup (2 oz) granulated sugar
- 2 teaspoons instant yeast (optional, for a quicker rise)
- 3 cups (13.5 oz) gluten-free all-purpose flour blend
- 1/2 cup (2oz) gluten-free oat flour
- 1/4 cup (1oz) psyllium husk powder
- 1 teaspoon baking powder
- 1 teaspoon salt
- 1/4 cup (2 oz) unsalted butter, melted (or dairy-free substitute)
- 1 large egg
- 1 teaspoon vanilla extract
- Oil for frying (such as vegetable oil or canola oil)

For the Glaze:

- 1 1/2 cups (6oz) powdered sugar
- 2-3 tablespoons milk (dairy or non-dairy)
- 1 teaspoon vanilla extract

INSTRUCTIONS:

1. **Prepare the Dough:**
- In a large mixing bowl, combine the gluten-free sourdough discard, warm milk, granulated sugar, and instant yeast (if using). Mix until well combined.
- Add the gluten-free all-purpose flour blend, gluten-free oat flour, psyllium husk powder, baking powder, and salt. Mix until a dough forms.
- Add the melted butter, egg, and vanilla extract. Knead the dough until smooth and elastic. If the dough is too sticky, add a little more flour as needed.
2. **First Rise:**
- Cover the mixing bowl with plastic wrap or a clean kitchen towel. Let the dough rise at room temperature for 4-6 hours, or until it has doubled in size.
3. **Shape the Donuts:**
- Once the dough has risen, turn it out onto a lightly floured surface. Roll the dough out to about 1/2-inch thickness.
- Use a donut cutter or round cookie cutters to cut out donut shapes. Place the cut donuts and donut holes on a baking sheet lined with parchment paper.
4. **Second Rise:**
- Cover the baking sheet with a clean kitchen towel and let the donuts rise for another 30-45 minutes, or until they have puffed up.
5. **Heat the Oil:**
- In a large pot or deep fryer, heat oil to 350°F (175°C).
6. **Fry the Donuts:**
- Carefully lower a few donuts at a time into the hot oil using a slotted spoon. Fry each donut for 1-2 minutes on each side, or until golden brown.
- Remove the donuts from the oil and place them on a cooling rack lined with paper towels to drain excess oil.
7. **Prepare the Glaze:**
- In a medium mixing bowl, whisk together the powdered sugar, milk, and vanilla extract until smooth.
8. **Glaze the Donuts:**
- While the donuts are still warm, dip each one into the glaze, allowing any excess to drip off.
- Place the glazed donuts back on the cooling rack to set.
9. **Serving:**
- Serve the donuts warm or at room temperature.
10. **Storage:**
- Store any leftover donuts in an airtight container at room temperature for up to 2 days. For longer storage, refrigerate for up to a week or freeze for up to 3 months. Reheat in the microwave or oven before serving.

INTERNATIONAL DELIGHTS

INDIAN NAAN

Calories 250; Fat 8 g; Carb 38 g; Protein 6 g

SERVINGS: 8

PREP TIME: 20 minutes   **RISING TIME:** 2-4 hours   **COOKING TIME:** 15-20 minutes

UTENSILS:

- Large mixing bowl
- Measuring cups and spoons
- Kitchen scale
- Rolling pin
- Cast iron skillet or non-stick pan
- Pastry brush
- Clean kitchen towel

INGREDIENTS:

- 1 cup (8 oz) sourdough discard
- 2 cups (9 oz) all-purpose flour
- 1/2 cup (4 oz) plain yogurt (dairy or non-dairy)
- 2 tablespoons olive oil
- 1 teaspoon baking powder
- 1/2 teaspoon baking soda
- 1 teaspoon salt
- 1 teaspoon sugar
- 1/4 cup (2 oz) warm water (if needed)

For Cooking:
- 2 tablespoons melted butter or ghee (for brushing)
- Optional toppings: garlic, fresh herbs, sesame seeds

INSTRUCTIONS:

1. **Prepare the Dough:**
- In a large mixing bowl, combine the sourdough discard, all-purpose flour, yogurt, olive oil, baking powder, baking soda, salt, and sugar.
- Mix until a soft dough forms. If the dough is too dry, add warm water a little at a time until the dough comes together.
- Knead the dough in the bowl or on a lightly floured surface for about 5 minutes until smooth and elastic.
2. **First Rise:**
- Cover the dough with a clean kitchen towel and let it rise at room temperature for 2-4 hours, or until it has doubled in size.
3. **Shape the Naan:**
- Once the dough has risen, divide it into 8 equal pieces.
- Roll each piece into a ball and then use a rolling pin to roll each ball into an oval or round shape about 1/4 inch thick.
4. **Preheat the Skillet:**
- Preheat a cast iron skillet or non-stick pan over medium-high heat.
5. **Cook the Naan:**
- Place one piece of rolled dough into the hot skillet. Cook for 1-2 minutes, or until bubbles form on the surface and the bottom is golden brown.
- Flip the naan and cook for another 1-2 minutes until the other side is golden brown.
- Remove the cooked naan from the skillet and place it on a plate. Cover with a clean kitchen towel to keep warm.
- Repeat with the remaining pieces of dough.
6. **Brush with Butter or Ghee:**
- While the naan is still warm, brush the top with melted butter or ghee. Add any optional toppings like garlic, fresh herbs, or sesame seeds.
7. **Serving:**
- Serve the naan warm with your favorite curries, dips, or as a side to any meal.
8. **Storage:**
- Store any leftover naan in an airtight container at room temperature for up to 2 days. For longer storage, refrigerate for up to a week or freeze for up to 3 months. Reheat in a skillet or microwave before serving.

SOURDOUGH ROTI

Calories 100; Fat 1 g; Carb 20 g; Protein 3 g

SERVINGS:
8

PREP TIME: 15 minutes	TIME FOR THE REST: 1 hour	COOKING TIME: 15-20 minutes

UTENSILS:

- Large mixing bowl
- Measuring cups and spoons
- Kitchen scale
- Rolling pin
- Cast iron skillet or non-stick pan
- Clean kitchen towel

INGREDIENTS:

- 1 cup (8 oz) sourdough discard
- 2 cups (9 oz) whole wheat flour or gluten-free all-purpose flour blend
- 2 tablespoons olive oil or melted butter
- 1/2 teaspoon salt
- 1/2 cup (4 oz) warm water (as needed)

INSTRUCTIONS:

1. **Prepare the Dough:**
- In a large mixing bowl, combine the sourdough discard, flour, olive oil or melted butter, and salt.
- Mix until a soft dough forms. Add warm water a little at a time if needed until the dough comes together.
- Knead the dough in the bowl or on a lightly floured surface for about 5 minutes until smooth and elastic.
2. **Resting:**
- Cover the dough with a clean kitchen towel and let it rest at room temperature for 1 hour.
3. **Shape the Roti:**
- Once the dough has rested, divide it into 8 equal pieces.
- Roll each piece into a ball and then use a rolling pin to roll each ball into a thin round shape about 1/8 inch thick.
4. **Preheat the Skillet:**
- Preheat a cast iron skillet or non-stick pan over medium-high heat.
5. **Cook the Roti:**
- Place one piece of rolled dough into the hot skillet. Cook for 1-2 minutes, or until bubbles form on the surface and the bottom is golden brown.
- Flip the roti and cook for another 1-2 minutes until the other side is golden brown.
- Remove the cooked roti from the skillet and place it on a plate. Cover with a clean kitchen towel to keep warm.
- Repeat with the remaining pieces of dough.
6. **Serving:**
- Serve the roti warm with your favorite curries, dips, or as a side to any meal.
7. **Storage:**
- Store any leftover roti in an airtight container at room temperature for up to 2 days. For longer storage, refrigerate for up to a week or freeze for up to 3 months. Reheat in a skillet or microwave before serving.

BAO BUNS

Calories 150; Fat 2 g; Carb 28 g; Protein 4 g

SERVINGS:
12

PREP TIME: 30 minutes	RISING TIME: 4-6 hours	COOKING TIME: 15-20 minutes

UTENSILS:

- Large mixing bowl
- Medium mixing bowl
- Measuring cups and spoons
- Kitchen scale
- Whisk
- Rolling pin
- Steamer basket
- Parchment paper
- Baking sheet
- Clean kitchen towel

INGREDIENTS:

- 1 cup (8 oz) sourdough discard
- 2 cups (9 oz) all-purpose flour
- 2 tablespoons sugar
- 1 teaspoon baking powder
- 1/2 teaspoon salt
- 2 tablespoons vegetable oil
- 1/2 cup (4 oz) warm water (as needed)

INSTRUCTIONS:

1. **Prepare the Dough:**
- In a large mixing bowl, combine the sourdough discard, all-purpose flour, sugar, baking powder, and salt.
- Add the vegetable oil and mix until a soft dough forms. Add warm water a little at a time if needed until the dough comes together.
- Knead the dough in the bowl or on a lightly floured surface for about 5 minutes until smooth and elastic.

2. **First Rise:**
- Cover the dough with a clean kitchen towel and let it rise at room temperature for 4-6 hours, or until it has doubled in size.

3. **Shape the Bao Buns:**
- Once the dough has risen, turn it out onto a lightly floured surface. Divide the dough into 12 equal pieces.
- Roll each piece into a ball and then use a rolling pin to roll each ball into an oval shape about 1/4 inch thick.
- Fold each oval in half to create the classic bao bun shape. Place each bun on a small piece of parchment paper.

4. **Second Rise:**
- Place the shaped buns on a baking sheet, cover with a clean kitchen towel, and let them rise for another 30-45 minutes, or until they have puffed up.

5. **Prepare the Steamer:**
- While the buns are rising, prepare your steamer basket. If using a bamboo steamer, line it with parchment paper or cabbage leaves to prevent sticking.

6. **Steam the Bao Buns:**
- Once the buns have risen, arrange them in the steamer basket, leaving some space between each bun to allow for expansion.
- Steam the buns over boiling water for 15-20 minutes, or until they are puffed up and cooked through.

7. **Serving:**
- Serve the bao buns warm with your favorite fillings such as braised pork, vegetables, or tofu.

8. **Storage:**
- Store any leftover bao buns in an airtight container in the refrigerator for up to 3 days. For longer storage, freeze the buns for up to 3 months. Reheat by steaming before serving.

EMPANADAS

Calories 300; Fat 15 g; Carb 32 g; Protein 8 g

SERVINGS: 12-14

PREP TIME: 30 minutes	CHILLING TIME: 1 hour	BAKING TIME: 25-30 minutes

UTENSILS:

- Large mixing bowl
- Measuring cups and spoons
- Kitchen scale
- Whisk
- Rolling pin
- Baking sheet
- Parchment paper
- Pastry brush

INGREDIENTS:

For the Dough:
- 1 cup (8 oz) sourdough discard
- 2 cups (9 oz) all-purpose flour
- 1/2 cup (4 oz) unsalted butter, cold and cubed
- 1 teaspoon salt
- 1 egg, beaten (for egg wash)
- Ice water (as needed)

For the Filling:
- 1/2 pound ground beef (or other filling of choice)
- 1 small onion, finely chopped
- 1 clove garlic, minced
- 1/2 teaspoon ground cumin
- 1/2 teaspoon paprika
- 1/4 teaspoon salt
- 1/4 teaspoon black pepper
- 1/4 cup (2 oz) raisins (optional)
- 1/4 cup (2 oz) green olives, chopped (optional)
- 1 hard-boiled egg, chopped (optional)
- 2 tablespoons olive oil

INSTRUCTIONS:

1. **Prepare the Dough:**
- In a large mixing bowl, combine the sourdough discard, all-purpose flour, and salt.
- Add the cold, cubed butter to the flour mixture. Use a pastry cutter or your fingers to cut the butter into the flour until the mixture resembles coarse crumbs.
- Add ice water, one tablespoon at a time, and mix until the dough comes together. Form the dough into a ball, wrap it in plastic wrap, and refrigerate for at least 1 hour.

2. **Prepare the Filling:**
- In a skillet, heat the olive oil over medium heat. Add the chopped onion and garlic, and sauté until translucent.
- Add the ground beef, cumin, paprika, salt, and black pepper. Cook until the beef is browned and cooked through.
- Stir in the raisins, green olives, and chopped hard-boiled egg (if using). Remove from heat and let the filling cool.

3. **Preheat the Oven:**
- Preheat your oven to 375°F (190°C). Line a baking sheet with parchment paper.

4. **Roll Out the Dough:**
- On a lightly floured surface, roll out the chilled dough to about 1/8-inch thickness.
- Use a round cutter or a glass to cut out circles of dough, about 4-6 inches in diameter.

5. **Fill the Empanadas:**
- Place a spoonful of the filling in the center of each dough circle.
- Fold the dough over the filling to create a half-moon shape. Press the edges together with a fork to seal.

6. **Prepare for Baking:**
- Place the filled empanadas on the prepared baking sheet.
- Brush the tops with the beaten egg to give them a golden color when baked.

7. **Bake the Empanadas:**
- Bake in the preheated oven for 25-30 minutes, or until the empanadas are golden brown.

8. **Serving:**
- Serve the empanadas warm with your favorite dipping sauce.

9. **Storage:**
- Store any leftover empanadas in an airtight container in the refrigerator for up to 3 days. Reheat in the oven or microwave before serving. Empanadas can also be frozen for up to 3 months.

PITA BREAD

Calories 130; Fat 1 g; Carb 26 g; Protein 5 g

SERVINGS:
8

PREP TIME: 20 minutes	RISING TIME: 2-4 hours	COOKING TIME: 10-15 minutes

UTENSILS:

- Large mixing bowl
- Measuring cups and spoons
- Kitchen scale
- Whisk
- Rolling pin
- Baking sheet or pizza stone
- Clean kitchen towel

INGREDIENTS:

- 1 cup (8 oz) sourdough discard
- 2 1/2 cups (11.25 oz) all-purpose flour
- 1/2 cup (4 oz) warm water
- 2 tablespoons olive oil
- 1 tablespoon honey or sugar
- 2 teaspoons salt
- 2 teaspoons instant yeast (optional, for a quicker rise)

INSTRUCTIONS:

1. **Prepare the Dough:**
- In a large mixing bowl, combine the sourdough discard, all-purpose flour, warm water, olive oil, honey or sugar, salt, and instant yeast (if using). Mix until a dough forms.
- Knead the dough in the bowl or on a lightly floured surface for about 5 minutes until smooth and elastic.
2. **First Rise:**
- Cover the dough with a clean kitchen towel and let it rise at room temperature for 2-4 hours, or until it has doubled in size.
3. **Preheat the Oven:**
- About 30 minutes before baking, preheat your oven to 450°F (230°C). Place a baking sheet or pizza stone in the oven to preheat as well.
4. **Shape the Pita Bread:**
- Once the dough has risen, turn it out onto a lightly floured surface. Divide the dough into 8 equal pieces.
- Roll each piece into a ball and then use a rolling pin to roll each ball into a circle about 1/4 inch thick.
5. **Bake the Pita Bread:**
- Carefully place the rolled-out dough onto the preheated baking sheet or pizza stone. Bake for 5-7 minutes, or until the pitas puff up and are lightly golden brown.
- Remove the pitas from the oven and cover them with a clean kitchen towel to keep them soft while you bake the remaining dough.
6. **Serving:**
- Serve the pita bread warm or at room temperature with your favorite dips, spreads, or fillings.
7. **Storage:**
- Store any leftover pita bread in an airtight container at room temperature for up to 2 days. For longer storage, refrigerate for up to a week or freeze for up to 3 months. Reheat in the oven or toaster before serving.

85

SOURDOUGH DUMPLINGS

Calories 180; Fat 8 g; Carb 10 g; Protein 7 g

SERVINGS:
24

PREP TIME: 30 minutes	RISING TIME: 1-2 hours	COOKING TIME: 15-20 minutes

UTENSILS:

- Large mixing bowl
- Measuring cups and spoons
- Kitchen scale
- Rolling pin
- Parchment paper
- Baking sheet
- Large pot or steamer

INGREDIENTS:

For the Dough:
- 1 cup (8 oz) sourdough discard
- 2 cups (9 oz) all-purpose flour
- 1/2 teaspoon salt
- 1/4 cup (2 oz) warm water (as needed)

For the Filling:
- 1/2 pound ground pork or chicken
- 1 cup (4 oz) finely chopped cabbage
- 2 green onions, finely chopped
- 1 tablespoon soy sauce
- 1 tablespoon sesame oil
- 1 tablespoon grated ginger
- 1 clove garlic, minced
- 1/2 teaspoon salt
- 1/4 teaspoon black pepper

INSTRUCTIONS:

1. **Prepare the Dough:**
- In a large mixing bowl, combine the sourdough discard, all-purpose flour, and salt.
- Add warm water a little at a time and mix until a soft dough forms. Knead the dough in the bowl or on a lightly floured surface for about 5 minutes until smooth and elastic.
- Cover the dough with a clean kitchen towel and let it rest for 1-2 hours.

2. **Prepare the Filling:**
- In a medium mixing bowl, combine the ground pork or chicken, chopped cabbage, green onions, soy sauce, sesame oil, grated ginger, minced garlic, salt, and black pepper. Mix until well combined.

3. **Shape the Dumplings:**
- Once the dough has rested, turn it out onto a lightly floured surface. Divide the dough into 24 equal pieces.
- Roll each piece into a ball and then use a rolling pin to roll each ball into a thin circle about 3-4 inches in diameter.
- Place a small spoonful of filling in the center of each dough circle. Fold the dough over the filling to create a half-moon shape and pinch the edges together to seal. You can also pleat the edges for a traditional dumpling look.

Cook the Dumplings:

4. **To Steam:**
- Place the dumplings on a piece of parchment paper in a steamer basket, making sure they are not touching. Steam over boiling water for 15-20 minutes, or until the filling is cooked through.

5. **To Boil:**
- Bring a large pot of water to a boil. Gently add the dumplings to the boiling water, being careful not to overcrowd the pot. Cook for 6-8 minutes, or until the dumplings float to the top and the filling is cooked through.

6. **To Pan-Fry:**
- Heat a tablespoon of oil in a large skillet over medium heat. Add the dumplings in a single layer and cook until the bottoms are golden brown, about 2-3 minutes. Add 1/4 cup of water to the skillet and cover. Cook for an additional 5-6 minutes, or until the filling is cooked through and the water has evaporated.

7. **Serving:**
- Serve the dumplings hot with soy sauce, vinegar, or your favorite dipping sauce.

8. **Storage:**
- Store any leftover dumplings in an airtight container in the refrigerator for up to 3 days. For longer storage, freeze the uncooked dumplings on a baking sheet until solid, then transfer to a freezer-safe bag. Cook from frozen as directed above.

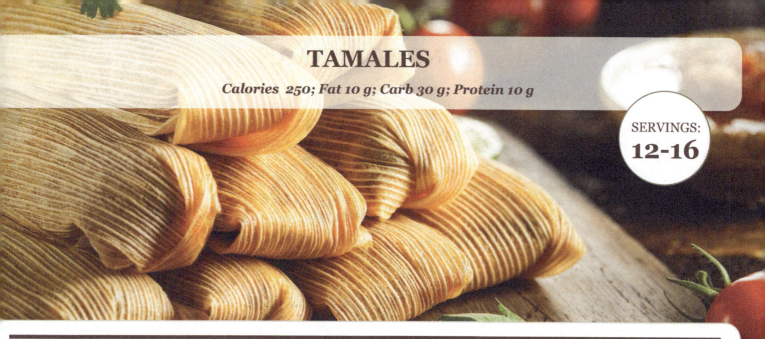

TAMALES

Calories 250; Fat 10 g; Carb 30 g; Protein 10 g

SERVINGS: 12-16

PREP TIME: 1 hours   COOKING TIME: 1-2 hours

UTENSILS:

- Large mixing bowl
- Measuring cups and spoons
- Kitchen scale
- Whisk
- Steamer pot or large pot with steamer basket
- Corn husks or parchment paper
- Mixer or hand whisk
- Spatula

INGREDIENTS:

For the Dough:
- 1 cup (8 oz) sourdough discard
- 2 cups (9 oz) masa harina (corn flour for tamales)
- 1 teaspoon baking powder
- 1/2 teaspoon salt
- 1/2 cup (4 oz) vegetable oil or melted lard
- 2 cups (16 oz) warm chicken or vegetable broth (or as needed)

For the Filling:
- 2 cups cooked and shredded chicken, pork, beef, or your preferred filling
- 1 cup (8 oz) salsa, mole, or your favorite sauce
- 1/2 cup (4 oz) shredded cheese (optional)

Other:
- Dried corn husks (soaked in warm water for 30 minutes) or parchment paper cut into rectangles

INSTRUCTIONS:

1. **Prepare the Corn Husks:**
- Soak the dried corn husks in warm water for about 30 minutes to make them pliable. If using parchment paper, cut it into rectangles approximately 8x10 inches.
2. **Prepare the Dough:**
- In a large mixing bowl, combine the masa harina, baking powder, and salt.
- Add the sourdough discard and vegetable oil or melted lard to the dry ingredients and mix well.
- Gradually add the warm broth, mixing with a hand whisk or mixer until the dough is smooth and spreadable but not too runny. The dough should have a consistency similar to thick peanut butter.
3. **Prepare the Filling:**
- In a medium mixing bowl, combine the shredded meat with the salsa or sauce. Add shredded cheese if using.
4. **Assemble the Tamales:**
- Lay a soaked corn husk (or parchment rectangle) flat on a clean surface. Spread about 1/4 cup of the dough onto the center of the husk, leaving about 1-2 inches at the bottom.
- Place a spoonful of the filling in the center of the dough.
- Fold the sides of the husk (or parchment) over the filling, then fold up the bottom end. If using parchment paper, you can tie the tamales with kitchen twine to keep them secure.
5. **Steam the Tamales:**
- Arrange the tamales in a steamer basket, standing them upright with the open ends facing up.
- Fill the bottom of the steamer pot with water, making sure it doesn't touch the tamales. Cover the pot with a lid.
- Steam the tamales over medium heat for 1-2 hours, or until the dough is firm and pulls away easily from the husk. Check occasionally to make sure there's enough water in the pot, adding more if needed.
6. **Serving:**
- Allow the tamales to cool slightly before serving. Serve with additional salsa, sour cream, or your favorite toppings.
7. **Storage:**
- Store any leftover tamales in an airtight container in the refrigerator for up to 5 days. For longer storage, freeze the tamales for up to 3 months. Reheat by steaming or microwaving before serving.

TANDOORI NAAN

Calories 260; Fat 8 g; Carb 40 g; Protein 7 g

PREP TIME: 20 minutes   **RISING TIME:** 2-4 hours   **COOKING TIME:** 15-20 minutes

UTENSILS:

- Large mixing bowl
- Measuring cups and spoons
- Kitchen scale
- Whisk
- Rolling pin
- Pastry brush
- Clean kitchen towel

INGREDIENTS:

- 1 cup (8 oz) sourdough discard
- 2 cups (9 oz) all-purpose flour
- 1/2 cup (4 oz) plain yogurt (dairy or non-dairy)
- 2 tablespoons olive oil
- 1 teaspoon baking powder
- 1/2 teaspoon baking soda
- 1 teaspoon salt
- 1 teaspoon sugar
- 1/4 cup (2 oz) warm water (if needed)
- 2 tablespoons melted butter or ghee (for brushing)
- Optional toppings: minced garlic, fresh herbs (such as cilantro), sesame seeds, nigella seeds

INSTRUCTIONS:

1. **Prepare the Dough:**
- In a large mixing bowl, combine the sourdough discard, all-purpose flour, yogurt, olive oil, baking powder, baking soda, salt, and sugar.
- Mix until a soft dough forms. If the dough is too dry, add warm water a little at a time until the dough comes together.
- Knead the dough in the bowl or on a lightly floured surface for about 5 minutes until smooth and elastic.
2. **First Rise:**
- Cover the dough with a clean kitchen towel and let it rise at room temperature for 2-4 hours, or until it has doubled in size.
3. **Shape the Naan:**
- Once the dough has risen, turn it out onto a lightly floured surface. Divide the dough into 8 equal pieces.
- Roll each piece into a ball and then use a rolling pin to roll each ball into an oval or round shape about 1/4 inch thick.
4. **Preheat the Oven:**
- Oven temperature: 475°F (245°C). While it preheats, place a pizza stone or baking sheet in the oven.
5. **Prepare for Baking:**
- Place the rolled-out naan dough onto a piece of parchment paper. For an extra crisp texture, lightly brush the top of each naan with water.
6. **Bake the Naan:**
- Carefully slide the naan (with the parchment paper) onto the baking sheet or hot pizza stone.
- Bake for 4-6 minutes, or until bubbles form and the naan is golden brown on top.
- For an extra charred effect, you can broil the naan for 1-2 minutes, watching closely to prevent burning.
7. **Brush with Butter or Ghee:**
- Remove the naan from the oven and immediately brush the top with melted butter or ghee. Additionally, optional toppings like minced garlic, fresh herbs, or seeds can be added at this stage.
8. **Serving:**
- Serve the naan warm with your favorite curries, dips, or as a side to any meal.
9. **Storage:**
- Store any leftover naan for up to two days at room temperature in an airtight container. Use the freezer for up to three months or the refrigerator for up to a week of extended storage. Reheat in the oven before serving.

PARATHA

Calories 300; Fat 15 g; Carb 38 g; Protein 6 g

SERVINGS: 8

PREP TIME: 20 minutes   **TIME FOR THE REST:** 1-2 hours   **COOKING TIME:** 20-25 minutes

UTENSILS:

- Large mixing bowl
- Measuring cups and spoons
- Kitchen scale
- Rolling pin
- Cast iron skillet or non-stick pan
- Pastry brush
- Clean kitchen towel

INGREDIENTS:

- 1 cup (8 oz) sourdough discard
- 2 cups (9 oz) whole wheat flour or all-purpose flour
- 1/2 cup (4 oz) plain yogurt (dairy or non-dairy)
- 2 tablespoons vegetable oil or ghee (clarified butter)
- 1 teaspoon salt
- 1/2 teaspoon sugar
- Warm water as needed
- Additional oil or ghee for cooking

Optional Fillings:
- Finely chopped herbs (such as cilantro or fenugreek leaves)
- Spices (such as cumin seeds, coriander powder, or chili flakes)
- Finely chopped vegetables (such as onions or spinach)

INSTRUCTIONS:

1. **Prepare the Dough:**
- In a large mixing bowl, combine the sourdough discard, whole wheat flour or all-purpose flour, yogurt, vegetable oil or ghee, salt, and sugar.
- Mix until a soft dough forms. If the dough is too dry, add warm water a little at a time until the dough comes together.
- Knead the dough in the bowl or on a lightly floured surface for about 5 minutes until smooth and elastic.
2. **Resting:**
- Cover the dough with a clean kitchen towel and let it rest at room temperature for 1 hour.
3. **Shape the Paratha:**
- Once the dough has rested, divide it into 8 equal pieces.
- Roll each piece into a ball. Flatten each ball slightly and, if using a filling, place a small amount of filling in the center. Fold the dough over the filling and pinch to seal.
- Roll each filled or plain ball into a circle about 1/4 inch thick.
4. **Preheat the Skillet:**
- Preheat a cast iron skillet or non-stick pan over medium-high heat.
5. **Cook the Paratha:**
- Place one rolled paratha onto the hot skillet. Cook for 1-2 minutes, or until bubbles form on the surface and the bottom is golden brown.
- Flip the paratha and brush the top with a little oil or ghee. Cook for another 1-2 minutes until the other side is golden brown.
- Remove the paratha from the skillet and place it on a plate. Cover with a clean kitchen towel to keep warm.
- Repeat with the remaining dough.
6. **Serving:**
- Serve the paratha warm with your favorite curries, chutneys, or yogurt.
7. **Storage:**
- Store any leftover paratha in an airtight container at room temperature for up to 2 days. For longer storage, refrigerate for up to a week or freeze for up to 3 months. Reheat in a skillet or microwave before serving.

SOURDOUGH CHAPATI

Calories 100; Fat 2 g; Carb 20 g; Protein 3 g

SERVINGS:
10-12

PREP TIME: 15 minutes   **TIME FOR THE REST:** 30 minutes   **COOKING TIME:** 20 minutes

UTENSILS:

- Large mixing bowl
- Measuring cups and spoons
- Kitchen scale
- Rolling pin
- Cast iron skillet or non-stick pan
- Clean kitchen towel

INGREDIENTS:

- 1 cup (8 oz) sourdough discard
- 2 cups (9 oz) whole wheat flour or all-purpose flour
- 1 tablespoon vegetable oil or melted ghee
- 1/2 teaspoon salt
- Warm water as needed

INSTRUCTIONS:

1. **Prepare the Dough:**
- In a large mixing bowl, combine the sourdough discard, whole wheat flour or all-purpose flour, vegetable oil or melted ghee, and salt.
- Mix until a soft dough forms. If the dough is too dry, add warm water a little at a time until the dough comes together.
- Knead the dough in the bowl or on a lightly floured surface for about 5 minutes until smooth and elastic.
2. **Resting:**
- Cover the dough with a clean kitchen towel and let it rest at room temperature for 30 minutes.
3. **Shape the Chapati:**
- Once the dough has rested, divide it into 10-12 equal pieces.
- Roll each piece into a ball. Using a rolling pin, roll each ball into a thin circle about 1/8 inch thick.
4. **Preheat the Skillet:**
- Preheat a cast iron skillet or non-stick pan over medium-high heat.
5. **Cook the Chapati:**
- Place one rolled chapati onto the hot skillet. Cook for 1-2 minutes, or until bubbles form on the surface and light brown spots appear on the bottom.
- Flip the chapati and cook for another 1-2 minutes until the other side has light brown spots and is cooked through.
- If desired, press the chapati gently with a clean kitchen towel or spatula to help it puff up.
- Remove the chapati from the skillet and place it on a plate. Cover with a clean kitchen towel to keep warm.
- Repeat with the remaining dough.
6. **Serving:**
- Serve the chapati warm with your favorite curries, vegetables, or any meal of your choice.
7. **Storage:**
- Store any leftover chapati in an airtight container at room temperature for up to 2 days. For longer storage, refrigerate for up to a week or freeze for up to 3 months. Reheat in a skillet or microwave before serving.

FERMENTED FOODS &
BEVERAGES

KIMCHI

Calories 20; Fat 1 g; Carb 6 g; Protein 3 g

**SERVINGS:
8-10**

PREP TIME: 45 minutes

FERMENTING TIME: 2-7 days

UTENSILS:

- Large mixing bowl
- Measuring cups and spoons
- Kitchen scale
- Knife and cutting board
- Colander
- Large jar or fermentation crock
- Clean kitchen towel or lid

INGREDIENTS:

- 1 medium Napa cabbage (about 2 pounds)
- 1/4 cup sea salt (for salting cabbage)
- 1 cup (8 oz) sourdough discard
- 1 cup (8 oz) water
- 1 tablespoon sea salt (for brine)
- 1 tablespoon sugar
- 1 tablespoon grated ginger
- 3-4 cloves garlic, minced
- 3-4 green onions, chopped
- 1 medium carrot, julienned
- 2-3 tablespoons Korean red pepper flakes (Gochugaru) (adjust to taste)
- 1 tablespoon fish sauce or soy sauce (optional)

INSTRUCTIONS:

1. **Prepare the Cabbage:**
- Cut the Napa cabbage lengthwise into quarters and then chop into bite-sized pieces.
- Place the cabbage pieces in a large mixing bowl and sprinkle with 1/4 cup of sea salt. Toss to combine, ensuring the salt is evenly distributed.
- Let the cabbage sit for 1-2 hours, tossing occasionally. The salt will draw out moisture from the cabbage, making it wilt.
2. **Rinse and Drain the Cabbage:**
- After the cabbage has wilted, rinse it thoroughly under cold water to remove the excess salt.
- Place the cabbage in a colander to drain for 10-15 minutes. Squeeze out any remaining water.
3. **Prepare the Kimchi Paste:**
- In a separate bowl, combine the sourdough discard, water, 1 tablespoon sea salt, sugar, grated ginger, minced garlic, Korean red pepper flakes, and fish sauce or soy sauce (if using). Mix well to form a thick paste.
4. **Combine Vegetables and Paste:**
- In a large mixing bowl, combine the drained cabbage, chopped green onions, and julienned carrot.
- Add the kimchi paste to the vegetables and use your hands (wearing gloves if desired) to thoroughly mix and coat the vegetables with the paste.
5. **Pack the Kimchi:**
- Pack the kimchi mixture tightly into a large jar or fermentation crock, pressing down to remove any air pockets.
- Leave some space at the top of the jar (about 1 inch) to allow for expansion during fermentation.
- Cover the jar with a clean kitchen towel or loosely with a lid to allow gases to escape.
6. **Fermentation:**
- Let the kimchi ferment at room temperature for 2-7 days, depending on your taste preference. Check the kimchi daily, pressing down to keep the vegetables submerged in the brine.
- Taste the kimchi after 2 days to see if it has reached your desired level of fermentation. It should be tangy and slightly fizzy.
7. **Serving:**
- Serve the kimchi as a snack, in salads, or as a tangy side dish.
8. **Storage:**
- Once the kimchi has fermented to your liking, transfer the jar to the refrigerator. The cool temperature will slow down the fermentation process.
- Kimchi can be stored in the refrigerator for several weeks, developing more flavor over time.

SAUERKRAUT

Calories 20; Fat 0 g; Carb 6 g; Protein 1 g

PREP TIME: 30 minutes

FERMENTING TIME: 1-4 weeks

UTENSILS:

- Large mixing bowl
- Measuring cups and spoons
- Kitchen scale
- Knife and cutting board
- Large jar or fermentation crock
- Clean kitchen towel or lid
- Fermentation weight or small jar (to keep cabbage submerged)

INGREDIENTS:

- 1 medium green cabbage (about 2 pounds)
- 1 tablespoon sea salt
- 1/4 cup (2 oz) sourdough discard
- 1 tablespoon caraway seeds (optional)

INSTRUCTIONS:

1. **Prepare the Cabbage:**
- Remove the outer leaves of the cabbage and set one large leaf aside.
- Cut the cabbage into quarters and remove the core. Thinly slice the cabbage into fine shreds.
2. **Salt the Cabbage:**
- Place the shredded cabbage in a large mixing bowl. Sprinkle the sea salt over the cabbage.
- Use your hands to massage the salt into the cabbage for about 5-10 minutes. The cabbage will start to soften and release its juices.
3. **Add the Sourdough Discard:**
- Add the sourdough discard to the cabbage and mix thoroughly. The discard will help kickstart the fermentation process.
4. **Pack the Cabbage:**
- Pack the cabbage tightly into a large jar or fermentation crock, pressing down firmly to remove any air pockets. Use the liquid released from the cabbage to cover it. If there's not enough liquid, add a little filtered water to ensure the cabbage is submerged.
- Place the reserved cabbage leaf on top of the shredded cabbage to keep it submerged. Add a fermentation weight or a small jar filled with water to keep the cabbage submerged under the brine.
5. **Fermentation:**
- Cover the jar with a clean kitchen towel or loosely with a lid to allow gases to escape.
- Let the sauerkraut ferment at room temperature, away from direct sunlight, for 1-4 weeks. Check the sauerkraut daily, pressing down to keep the cabbage submerged in the brine.
6. **Serving:**
- Serve the sauerkraut as a snack, in salads, or as a tangy side dish.
7. **Taste and Store:**
- Start tasting the sauerkraut after one week. When it reaches your desired level of tanginess, transfer the jar to the refrigerator to slow down the fermentation process.
- Sauerkraut can be stored in the refrigerator for several months, continuing to develop flavor over time.

PICKLES

Calories 12; Fat 0 g; Carb 3 g; Protein 0 g

PREP TIME: 20 minutes   **FERMENTING TIME: 3-7 days**

UTENSILS:

- Large mixing bowl
- Measuring cups and spoons
- Kitchen scale
- Knife and cutting board
- Large jar or fermentation crock
- Clean kitchen towel or lid
- Fermentation weight or small jar (to keep cucumbers submerged)

INGREDIENTS:

- 1 pound cucumbers (small pickling cucumbers or sliced cucumbers)
- 1/4 cup (2 oz) sourdough discard
- 2 tablespoons sea salt
- 2 cups (16 oz) water (non-chlorinated)
- 2-3 cloves garlic, smashed
- 1 tablespoon dill seeds or fresh dill sprigs
- 1 teaspoon black peppercorns
- 1 teaspoon mustard seeds (optional)
- 1/2 teaspoon red pepper flakes (optional)

INSTRUCTIONS:

1. **Prepare the Brine:**
- In a large mixing bowl, combine the sea salt and water. Stir until the salt is fully dissolved to make a brine.
- Add the sourdough discard to the brine and mix well.
2. **Prepare the Cucumbers:**
- Wash the cucumbers thoroughly and slice off the blossom end to prevent bitterness. You can leave the cucumbers whole, slice them into spears, or cut them into rounds.
3. **Pack the Jar:**
- Place the smashed garlic cloves, dill seeds or sprigs, black peppercorns, mustard seeds (if using), and red pepper flakes (if using) at the bottom of a large jar or fermentation crock.
- Pack the cucumbers tightly into the jar, leaving about 1 inch of headspace at the top.
4. **Add the Brine:**
- Pour the brine over the cucumbers, ensuring they are fully submerged. If necessary, add more water to cover the cucumbers.
- Place a fermentation weight or a small jar filled with water on top of the cucumbers to keep them submerged under the brine.
5. **Fermentation:**
- Cover the jar with a clean kitchen towel or loosely with a lid to allow gases to escape.
- Let the pickles ferment at room temperature, away from direct sunlight, for 3-7 days. Check the pickles daily, ensuring they stay submerged and skimming off any surface scum if it forms.
6. **Serving:**
- Serve the pickles as a snack, in salads, or as a tangy side dish.
7. **Taste and Store:**
- Start tasting the pickles after 3 days. When they reach your desired level of tanginess and crunch, transfer the jar to the refrigerator to slow down the fermentation process.
- The pickles can be stored in the refrigerator for several months, continuing to develop flavor over time.

KOMBUCHA

Calories 30; Fat 0 g; Carb 10 g; Protein 0 g

PREP TIME: 30 minutes   **FERMENTING TIME:** 7-10 days for primary fermentation, 3-5 days for secondary fermentation

UTENSILS:

- Large pot
- Measuring cups and spoons
- Kitchen scale
- Whisk
- 1-gallon glass jar
- Clean kitchen towel or coffee filter
- Rubber band
- Bottles for secondary fermentation (if desired)

INGREDIENTS:

- 1 cup (8 oz) sourdough discard
- 1 SCOBY (Symbiotic Culture of Bacteria and Yeast)
- 1 cup (8 oz) sugar
- 8 cups (64 oz) water
- 4-6 bags of black or green tea (or 1-2 tablespoons loose leaf tea)
- 1 cup (8 oz) starter kombucha (from a previous batch or store-bought raw kombucha)

For Secondary Fermentation (Optional):
- Fruit juice, fresh fruit, or herbs for flavoring

INSTRUCTIONS:

1. **Prepare the Sweet Tea:**
- Bring the water to a boil in a large pot. Remove from heat and add the tea bags or loose leaf tea. Let it steep for 10 minutes.
- Remove the tea bags or strain out the loose tea leaves.
- Stir in the sugar until fully dissolved. Allow the sweet tea to cool to room temperature.
2. **Mix the Sourdough Discard:**
- In a medium bowl, whisk together the sourdough discard with a little bit of the cooled sweet tea until smooth. This helps to incorporate the discard into the kombucha.
3. **Combine Ingredients:**
- In the 1-gallon glass jar, combine the cooled sweet tea, sourdough discard mixture, and starter kombucha.
- Gently place the SCOBY on top of the liquid. It may sink or float, either is fine.
4. **Primary Fermentation:**
- Cover the jar with a clean kitchen towel or coffee filter and secure it with a rubber band.
- Place the jar in a warm, dark place 70-75°F (21-24°C) for 7-10 days. The fermentation time can vary based on temperature and personal taste preferences. Taste the kombucha starting at 7 days and continue fermenting until it reaches your desired flavor.
5. **Secondary Fermentation (Optional):**
- For a fizzy kombucha, you can proceed with a secondary fermentation. Pour the kombucha (reserving the SCOBY and 1 cup of kombucha for your next batch) into bottles, leaving about 1 inch of headspace.
- Add fruit juice, fresh fruit, or herbs (such as chamomile, thyme, or oregano) to each bottle for flavor. Cap bottles tightly.
- Let the bottles sit at room temperature for 3-5 days. Check the carbonation level by opening a bottle after 3 days. Once it's to your liking, refrigerate the bottles to slow down the fermentation process.
6. **Serving:**
- Once chilled, your kombucha is ready to drink. Pour it into a glass and enjoy!
7. **Storage:**
- Store the finished kombucha in the refrigerator. It can be kept for several weeks, but the flavor may continue to develop over time.

KEFIR

Calories 125; Fat 5 g; Carb 23 g; Protein 8 g

PREP TIME: 10 minutes

FERMENTING TIME: 24-48 hours

UTENSILS:

- Large mixing bowl
- Measuring cups and spoons
- Kitchen scale
- Whisk
- Large glass jar or fermentation vessel
- Cheesecloth or clean kitchen towel
- Rubber band
- Strainer

INGREDIENTS:

- 1 cup (8 oz) sourdough discard
- 4 cups (32 oz) milk (dairy or non-dairy)
- 2 tablespoons kefir grains (available online or at health food stores)

INSTRUCTIONS:

1. **Prepare the Fermentation Vessel:**
- In a large mixing bowl, whisk together the sourdough discard with a little bit of the milk until smooth.
- Pour the mixture into a large glass jar or fermentation vessel.
- Add the remaining milk to the jar and stir gently to combine.

2. **Add the Kefir Grains:**
- Add the kefir grains to the milk mixture. Stir gently to distribute the grains evenly.

3. **Cover and Ferment:**
- Cover the jar with cheesecloth or a clean kitchen towel and secure it with a rubber band to keep out dust and insects.
- Place the jar in a warm, dark place 68-78°F (20-26°C) for 24-48 hours. The fermentation time can vary based on temperature and personal taste preferences. Stir the mixture gently once or twice a day to keep the grains well-distributed.

4. **Check for Doneness:**
- After 24 hours, check the kefir for taste and consistency. It should be slightly thickened and tangy. If you prefer a stronger flavor, allow it to ferment for up to 48 hours.

5. **Strain the Kefir:**
- Once the kefir has reached your desired flavor, strain it through a fine mesh strainer into a clean bowl or jar to remove the kefir grains.
- Set the kefir grains aside for your next batch. They can be stored in a small amount of fresh milk in the refrigerator for up to a week.

6. **Transfer and Store:**
- Transfer the strained kefir to a clean jar or bottle and refrigerate it. It will continue to thicken and develop flavor in the refrigerator.
- Store the kefir in the refrigerator for up to 2 weeks.

7. **Serving:**
- Serve the kefir chilled. You can drink it plain or add fruit, honey, or other flavorings as desired.

FERMENTED HOT SAUCE

Calories 10; Fat 0 g; Carb 5 g; Protein 0 g

PREP TIME: 20 minutes   **FERMENTING TIME:** 1-2 weeks

UTENSILS:

- Large mixing bowl
- Measuring cups and spoons
- Kitchen scale
- Knife and cutting board
- Blender or food processor
- Large jar or fermentation crock
- Clean kitchen towel or coffee filter
- Rubber band
- Fine mesh strainer
- Bottles for storage

INGREDIENTS:

- 1 cup (8 oz) sourdough discard
- 2 cups (16 oz) hot peppers (such as jalapeños, habaneros, or a mix), stems removed and chopped
- 4 cloves garlic, peeled and chopped
- 1 small onion, chopped
- 1 tablespoon sea salt
- 2 cups (16 oz) water (non-chlorinated)

INSTRUCTIONS:

1. **Prepare the Brine:**
- In a large mixing bowl, combine the sea salt and water. Stir until the salt is fully dissolved to make a brine.
2. **Prepare the Vegetables:**
- Wash and chop the hot peppers, garlic, and onion. Wear gloves if handling very hot peppers to avoid skin irritation.
3. **Mix the Ingredients:**
- In a large jar or fermentation crock, combine the chopped peppers, garlic, and onion.
- Add the sourdough discard and pour the brine over the vegetables, ensuring they are fully submerged. If necessary, add more water to keep the vegetables submerged.
4. **Cover and Ferment:**
- Cover the jar with a clean kitchen towel or coffee filter and secure it with a rubber band to keep out dust and insects.
- Place the jar in a cool, dark place 65-75°F (18-24°C) for 1-2 weeks. Check the mixture daily to ensure the vegetables remain submerged, and skim off any surface mold or scum if it forms.
5. **Blend the Sauce:**
- After 1-2 weeks, the mixture should have a tangy, slightly sour smell and taste. Transfer the mixture to a blender or food processor and blend until smooth.
6. **Strain the Sauce:**
- Pour the blended mixture through a fine mesh strainer into a bowl, pressing down with a spoon to extract as much liquid as possible. Discard the solids.
7. **Bottle and Store:**
- Transfer the strained hot sauce to clean bottles. Seal tightly and refrigerate. The flavor will continue to develop over time.
8. **Serving:**
- Use the fermented hot sauce as a condiment on your favorite dishes. Shake well before each use.

FERMENTED VEGETABLES

Calories 20; Fat 0 g; Carb 4 g; Protein 1 g

SERVINGS: 8-10

PREP TIME: 30 minutes   **FERMENTING TIME:** 1-2 weeks

UTENSILS:

- Large mixing bowl
- Measuring cups and spoons
- Kitchen scale
- Knife and cutting board
- Large jar or fermentation crock
- Clean kitchen towel or coffee filter
- Rubber band
- Fermentation weight or small jar (to keep vegetables submerged)

INGREDIENTS:

- 1 cup (8 oz) sourdough discard
- 2 pounds mixed vegetables (such as carrots, cucumbers, bell peppers, radishes, or cauliflower), washed and chopped
- 4 cloves garlic, peeled and smashed
- 1 small onion, chopped
- 2 tablespoons sea salt
- 2-3 cups (16-24 oz) water (non-chlorinated)

Optional Seasonings:
- Fresh herbs (such as dill, thyme, or oregano)
- Whole spices (such as peppercorns, mustard seeds, or coriander seeds)
- Red pepper flakes (for a spicy kick)

INSTRUCTIONS:

1. **Prepare the Brine:**
- In a large mixing bowl, combine the sea salt and water. Stir until the salt is fully dissolved to make a brine.
2. **Prepare the Vegetables:**
- Wash and chop the mixed vegetables into bite-sized pieces. Smash the garlic cloves and chop the onion.
3. **Mix the Ingredients:**
- In a large jar or fermentation crock, combine the chopped vegetables, garlic, and onion.
- Add any optional seasonings you desire.
- Pour the sourdough discard over the vegetables and then pour the brine over the mixture, ensuring the vegetables are fully submerged. If necessary, add more water to keep the vegetables submerged.
4. **Cover and Ferment:**
- Place a fermentation weight or a small jar filled with water on top of the vegetables to keep them submerged under the brine.
- Cover the jar with a clean kitchen towel or coffee filter and secure it with a rubber band to keep out dust and insects.
- Place the jar in a cool, dark place 65-75°F (18-24°C) for 1-2 weeks. Check the mixture daily to ensure the vegetables remain submerged, and skim off any surface mold or scum if it forms.
5. **Taste and Store:**
- Start tasting the vegetables after 1 week. When they reach your desired level of tanginess and crunch, transfer the jar to the refrigerator to slow down the fermentation process.
- The fermented vegetables can be stored in the refrigerator for several months, continuing to develop flavor over time.
6. **Serving:**
- Serve the fermented vegetables as a side dish, in salads, or as a topping for sandwiches and tacos.

SOURDOUGH DISCARD FERMENTED SALSA

Calories 12; Fat 0 g; Carb 4 g; Protein 0 g

PREP TIME: 20 minutes

FERMENTING TIME: 2-4 days

UTENSILS:

- Large mixing bowl
- Measuring cups and spoons
- Kitchen scale
- Knife and cutting board
- Large jar or fermentation crock
- Clean kitchen towel or coffee filter
- Rubber band

INGREDIENTS:

- 1 cup (8 oz) sourdough discard
- 2 pounds tomatoes, finely chopped
- 1 large onion, finely chopped
- 3-4 cloves garlic, minced
- 2-3 jalapeño peppers, finely chopped (adjust to taste)
- 1/2 cup fresh cilantro, chopped
- Juice of 2 limes
- 1 tablespoon sea salt
- 1 teaspoon ground cumin (optional)
- 1 teaspoon black pepper

INSTRUCTIONS:

1. **Prepare the Vegetables:**
- Wash and finely chop the tomatoes, onion, garlic, jalapeño peppers, and cilantro.
2. **Mix the Ingredients:**
- In a large mixing bowl, combine the chopped tomatoes, onion, garlic, jalapeños, and cilantro.
- Add the sourdough discard, lime juice, sea salt, ground cumin (if using), and black pepper. Mix well to combine.
3. **Pack the Jar:**
- Transfer the salsa mixture to a large jar or fermentation crock. Press down firmly to remove any air pockets and ensure the vegetables are submerged in their own juices. Leave about 1 inch of headspace at the top of the jar.
4. **Cover and Ferment:**
- Cover the jar with a clean kitchen towel or coffee filter and secure it with a rubber band to keep out dust and insects.
- Place the jar in a cool, dark place 65-75°F (18-24°C) for 2-4 days. Check the salsa daily, pressing down to keep the vegetables submerged in the liquid.
5. **Taste and Store:**
- Start tasting the salsa after 2 days. When it reaches your desired level of tanginess, transfer the jar to the refrigerator to slow down the fermentation process.
- The fermented salsa can be stored in the refrigerator for up to 2 weeks.
6. **Serving:**
- Serve the fermented salsa with chips, tacos, burritos, or as a topping for grilled meats and vegetables.

FERMENTED CARROTS

Calories 25; Fat 0 g; Carb 6 g; Protein 1 g

SERVINGS: 6-8

PREP TIME: 20 minutes   **FERMENTING TIME:** 5-10 days

UTENSILS:

- Large mixing bowl
- Measuring cups and spoons
- Kitchen scale
- Knife and cutting board
- Large jar or fermentation crock
- Clean kitchen towel or coffee filter
- Rubber band
- Fermentation weight or small jar (to keep carrots submerged)

INGREDIENTS:

- 1 cup (8 oz) sourdough discard
- 1 pound carrots, peeled and cut into sticks or rounds
- 3 cloves garlic, smashed
- 1 tablespoon sea salt
- 2 cups (16 oz) water (non-chlorinated)
- 1 teaspoon whole black peppercorns (optional)
- 1 teaspoon mustard seeds (optional)
- 1-2 sprigs fresh dill or 1 teaspoon dried dill (optional)

INSTRUCTIONS:

1. **Prepare the Brine:**
- In a large mixing bowl, combine the sea salt and water. Stir until the salt is fully dissolved to make a brine.
2. **Prepare the Carrots:**
- Peel the carrots and cut them into sticks or rounds, depending on your preference.
3. **Mix the Ingredients:**
- In a large jar or fermentation crock, place the smashed garlic cloves, peppercorns, mustard seeds, and dill if using.
- Pack the carrots tightly into the jar, leaving about 1 inch of headspace at the top.
- Pour the sourdough discard over the carrots.
4. **Add the Brine:**
- Pour the brine over the carrots, ensuring they are fully submerged. If necessary, add more water to keep the carrots submerged.
5. **Cover and Ferment:**
- Place a fermentation weight or a small jar filled with water on top of the carrots to keep them submerged under the brine.
- Cover the jar with a clean kitchen towel or coffee filter and secure it with a rubber band to keep out dust and insects.
- Place the jar in a cool, dark place 65-75°F (18-24°C) for 5-10 days. Check the carrots daily, ensuring they stay submerged, and skim off any surface mold or scum if it forms.
6. **Taste and Store:**
- Start tasting the carrots after 5 days. When they reach your desired level of tanginess and crunch, transfer the jar to the refrigerator to slow down the fermentation process.
- The fermented carrots can be stored in the refrigerator for several months, continuing to develop flavor over time.
7. **Serving:**
- Serve the fermented carrots as a snack, in salads, or as a tangy side dish.

FERMENTED BEETS

Calories 35; Fat 0 g; Carb 8 g; Protein 1 g

SERVINGS: 8-10

PREP TIME: 30 minutes   **FERMENTING TIME:** 7-10 days

UTENSILS:

- Large mixing bowl
- Measuring cups and spoons
- Kitchen scale
- Knife and cutting board
- Large jar or fermentation crock
- Clean kitchen towel or coffee filter
- Rubber band
- Fermentation weight or small jar (to keep beets submerged)

INGREDIENTS:

- 1 cup (8 oz) sourdough discard
- 2 pounds beets, peeled and cut into thin slices or cubes
- 3 cloves garlic, smashed
- 1 tablespoon sea salt
- 4 cups (32 oz) water (non-chlorinated)
- 1 teaspoon whole black peppercorns (optional)
- 1 teaspoon mustard seeds (optional)
- 1-2 sprigs fresh dill or 1 teaspoon dried dill (optional)

INSTRUCTIONS:

1. **Prepare the Brine:**
- In a large mixing bowl, combine the sea salt and water. Stir until the salt is fully dissolved to make a brine.
2. **Prepare the Beets:**
- Peel the beets and cut them into thin slices or cubes, depending on your preference.
3. **Mix the Ingredients:**
- In a large jar or fermentation crock, place the smashed garlic cloves, peppercorns, mustard seeds, and dill if using.
- Pack the beets tightly into the jar, leaving about 1 inch of headspace at the top.
- Pour the sourdough discard over the beets.
4. **Add the Brine:**
- Pour the brine over the beets, ensuring they are fully submerged. If necessary, add more water to keep the beets submerged.
5. **Cover and Ferment:**
- Place a fermentation weight or a small jar filled with water on top of the beets to keep them submerged under the brine.
- Cover the jar with a clean kitchen towel or coffee filter and secure it with a rubber band to keep out dust and insects.
- Place the jar in a cool, dark place 65-75°F (18-24°C) for 7-10 days. Check the beets daily, ensuring they stay submerged, and skim off any surface mold or scum if it forms.
6. **Taste and Store:**
- Start tasting the beets after 7 days. When they reach your desired level of tanginess and texture, transfer the jar to the refrigerator to slow down the fermentation process.
- The fermented beets can be stored in the refrigerator for several months, continuing to develop flavor over time.
7. **Serving:**
- Serve the fermented beets as a side dish, in salads, or as a tangy addition to sandwiches and wraps.

SPECIAL OCCASION
RECIPES

HOLIDAY BREAD

Calories 200; Fat 6 g; Carb 32 g; Protein 4 g

SERVINGS:
10-12

PREP TIME: 30 minutes | RISING TIME: 4-6 hours | BAKING TIME: 35-40 minutes

UTENSILS:

- Large mixing bowl
- Measuring cups and spoons
- Kitchen scale
- Whisk
- Baking sheet or loaf pan
- Parchment paper
- Pastry brush
- Clean kitchen towel

INGREDIENTS:

- 1 cup (8 oz) sourdough discard
- 3 cups (13.5 oz) all-purpose flour
- 1/4 cup (2 oz) granulated sugar
- 1/2 cup (4 oz) warm milk (dairy or non-dairy)
- 1/4 cup (2 oz) unsalted butter, melted (or dairy-free substitute)
- 2 large eggs
- 1 teaspoon salt
- 1 teaspoon vanilla extract
- 1/2 cup (4 oz) dried fruit (such as cranberries, raisins, or currants)
- 1/2 cup (2 oz) chopped nuts (such as walnuts, pecans, or almonds)
- 1 teaspoon ground cinnamon (optional)
- Zest of 1 orange (optional)
- 1 egg, beaten (for egg wash)
- Powdered sugar for dusting (optional)

INSTRUCTIONS:

1. **Prepare the Dough:**
- In a large mixing bowl, whisk together the sourdough discard, warm milk, melted butter, granulated sugar, eggs, and vanilla extract until well combined.
- Add the all-purpose flour, salt, and ground cinnamon (if using). Mix until a soft dough forms.
- Knead the dough on a lightly floured surface for about 5-7 minutes until smooth and elastic.
2. **First Rise:**
- Place the dough back into the mixing bowl, cover with a clean kitchen towel, and let it rise at room temperature for 4-6 hours, or until it has doubled in size.
3. **Prepare the Add-ins:**
- While the dough is rising, prepare the dried fruit, chopped nuts, and orange zest (if using).
4. **Incorporate the Add-ins:**
- Once the dough has risen, turn it out onto a lightly floured surface. Gently knead in the dried fruit, chopped nuts, and orange zest until evenly distributed.
5. **Shape the Dough:**
- Shape the dough into a round or oval loaf. If using a loaf pan, shape the dough to fit the pan. Place the shaped dough onto a parchment-lined baking sheet or into the loaf pan.
6. **Second Rise:**
- Cover the dough with a clean kitchen towel and let it rise for another 1-2 hours, or until it has puffed up and holds an indentation when gently pressed.
7. **Preheat the Oven:**
- About 30 minutes before baking, preheat your oven to 350°F (175°C).
8. **Apply the Egg Wash:**
- Brush the top of the dough with the beaten egg to give it a golden color when baked.
9. **Bake the Bread:**
- Bake in the preheated oven for 35-40 minutes, or until the bread is golden brown and sounds hollow when tapped on the bottom. If the top browns too quickly, cover it loosely with aluminum foil.
10. **Cooling:**
- Remove the bread from the oven and let it cool on a wire rack.
11. **Serving:**
- Dust the cooled bread with powdered sugar before serving, if desired. Slice and enjoy!
12. **Storage:**
- Store any leftover bread in an airtight container at room temperature for up to 3 days. For longer storage, freeze the bread for up to 3 months. Reheat slices in the toaster or oven before serving.

103

BIRTHDAY CAKE

Calories 350; Fat 15 g; Carb 50 g; Protein 4 g

SERVINGS:
12-16

| PREP TIME: 30 minutes | BAKING TIME: 30-35 minutes | COOLING TIME: 1 hour |

UTENSILS:

- Large mixing bowl
- Measuring cups and spoons
- Kitchen scale
- Whisk
- Two 9-inch round cake pans
- Parchment paper
- Cooling rack
- Offset spatula (for frosting)

INGREDIENTS:

For the Cake:
- 1 cup (8 oz) sourdough discard
- 2 1/2 cups (11.25 oz) all-purpose flour
- 1 1/2 cups (12 oz) granulated sugar
- 1/2 cup (4 oz) unsalted butter, softened (or dairy-free substitute)
- 1/2 cup (4 oz) vegetable oil
- 1 cup (8 oz) milk (dairy or non-dairy)
- 3 large eggs
- 2 teaspoons vanilla extract
- 2 1/2 teaspoons baking powder
- 1/2 teaspoon baking soda
- 1/2 teaspoon salt

For the Frosting:
- 1 cup (8 oz) unsalted butter, softened (or dairy-free substitute)
- 4 cups (16 oz) powdered sugar
- 1/4 cup (2 oz) milk (dairy or non-dairy)
- 2 teaspoons vanilla extract
- Food coloring (optional)
- Sprinkles (optional, for decoration)

INSTRUCTIONS:

1. **Preheat the Oven:**
- Preheat your oven to 350°F (175°C). Grease and line two 9-inch round cake pans with parchment paper.

2. **Prepare the Cake Batter:**
- In a large mixing bowl, cream together the softened butter, vegetable oil, and granulated sugar until light and fluffy.
- Add the eggs one at a time, beating well after each addition. Stir in the vanilla extract and sourdough discard until well combined.
- In a separate bowl, whisk together the flour, baking powder, baking soda, and salt.
- Gradually add the dry ingredients to the wet ingredients, alternating with the milk, beginning and ending with the dry ingredients. Mix until just combined.

3. **Bake the Cakes:**
- Divide the batter evenly between the prepared cake pans and smooth the tops with a spatula.
- Bake in the preheated oven for 30-35 minutes, or until a toothpick inserted into the center of the cakes comes out clean.
- Remove the cakes from the oven and let them cool in the pans for 10 minutes. Then, transfer the cakes to a cooling rack to cool completely.

4. **Prepare the Frosting:**
- In a large mixing bowl, beat the softened butter until creamy.
- Gradually add the powdered sugar, 1 cup at a time, beating well after each addition.
- Add the milk and vanilla extract, and beat until the frosting is light and fluffy.
- If desired, divide the frosting into separate bowls and add food coloring to each bowl to create different colors.

5. **Assemble the Cake:**
- Once the cakes are completely cool, place one cake layer on a serving plate or cake stand.
- Spread a layer of frosting over the top of the first cake layer.
- Place the second cake layer on top of the frosting.
- Frost the top and sides of the cake with the remaining frosting, using an offset spatula to create a smooth finish.

6. **Decorate:**
- Decorate the cake with sprinkles, additional frosting designs, or other decorations as desired.

7. **Serving:**
- Slice and serve the cake at room temperature.

8. **Storage:**
- Store any leftover cake in an airtight container at room temperature for up to 3 days. For longer storage, refrigerate the cake for up to a week or freeze for up to 3 months. Bring to room temperature before serving.

FESTIVE ROLLS

Calories 150; Fat 4 g; Carb 25 g; Protein 4 g

PREP TIME: 20 minutes　　　　**RISING TIME:** 4-6 hours　　　　**BAKING TIME:** 20-25 minutes

UTENSILS:

- Large mixing bowl
- Measuring cups and spoons
- Kitchen scale
- Whisk
- Baking sheet or baking dish
- Parchment paper
- Pastry brush
- Clean kitchen towel

INGREDIENTS:

- 1 cup (8 oz) sourdough discard
- 3 cups (13.5 oz) all-purpose flour
- 1/4 cup (2 oz) granulated sugar
- 1/2 cup (4 oz) warm milk (dairy or non-dairy)
- 1/4 cup (2 oz) unsalted butter, melted (or dairy-free substitute)
- 2 large eggs
- 1 teaspoon salt
- 2 teaspoons instant yeast (optional, for a quicker rise)
- 1/2 teaspoon ground cinnamon (optional)
- 1/4 cup (2 oz) dried cranberries or raisins (optional)
- 1/4 cup (2 oz) chopped nuts (optional)
- 1 egg, beaten (for egg wash)
- Powdered sugar for dusting (optional)

INSTRUCTIONS:

1. **Prepare the Dough:**
- In a large mixing bowl, whisk together the sourdough discard, warm milk, melted butter, granulated sugar, and eggs until well combined.
- Add the all-purpose flour, salt, ground cinnamon (if using), and instant yeast (if using). Mix until a soft dough forms.
- Knead the dough on a lightly floured surface for about 5-7 minutes until smooth and elastic.
2. **First Rise:**
- Place the dough back into the mixing bowl, cover with a clean kitchen towel, and let it rise at room temperature for 4-6 hours, or until it has doubled in size.
3. **Prepare the Add-ins:**
- While the dough is rising, prepare the dried cranberries or raisins and chopped nuts (if using).
4. **Incorporate the Add-ins:**
- Once the dough has risen, turn it out onto a lightly floured surface. Gently knead in the dried cranberries or raisins and chopped nuts until evenly distributed.
5. **Shape the Rolls:**
- Divide the dough into 12 equal pieces.
- Roll each piece into a ball and place them on a parchment-lined baking sheet or baking dish.
6. **Second Rise:**
- Cover the rolls with a clean kitchen towel and let them rise for another 1-2 hours, or until they have puffed up and hold an indentation when gently pressed.
7. **Preheat the Oven:**
- About 30 minutes before baking, preheat your oven to 375°F (190°C).
8. **Apply the Egg Wash:**
- Brush the tops of the rolls with the beaten egg to give them a golden color when baked.
9. **Bake the Rolls:**
- Bake in the preheated oven for 20-25 minutes, or until the rolls are golden brown and sound hollow when tapped on the bottom.
10. **Cooling:**
- Remove the rolls from the oven and let them cool on a wire rack.
11. **Serving:**
- Dust the cooled rolls with powdered sugar before serving, if desired. Serve warm or at room temperature.
12. **Storage:**
- Store any leftover rolls in an airtight container at room temperature for up to 3 days. For longer storage, freeze the rolls for up to 3 months. Reheat in the oven or microwave before serving.

YULE LOG

Calories 300; Fat 15 g; Carb 40 g; Protein 5 g

SERVINGS:
8-10

| PREP TIME: 30 minutes | RISING TIME: 12-15 minutes | COOLING TIME: 1 hour |

UTENSILS:

- Large mixing bowl
- Measuring cups and spoons
- Kitchen scale
- Whisk
- Electric mixer
- Baking sheet (10x15 inch) with rim
- Parchment paper
- Clean kitchen towel
- Offset spatula

INGREDIENTS:

For the Cake:
- 1/2 cup (4 oz) sourdough discard
- 3/4 cup (3.25 oz) all-purpose flour
- 1/4 cup (1 oz) cocoa powder
- 1 teaspoon baking powder
- 1/4 teaspoon salt
- 4 large eggs
- 3/4 cup (6 oz) granulated sugar
- 1 teaspoon vanilla extract
- Powdered sugar for dusting

For the Filling:
- 1 cup (8 oz) heavy whipping cream
- 1/4 cup (2 oz) powdered sugar
- 1 teaspoon vanilla extract

For the Frosting:
- 1/2 cup (4 oz) unsalted butter, softened
- 1 1/2 cups (6 oz) powdered sugar
- 1/4 cup (1 oz) cocoa powder
- 1 teaspoon vanilla extract
- 2-3 tablespoons milk

INSTRUCTIONS:

1. **Preheat the Oven:**
- Preheat your oven to 350°F (175°C). Grease a 10x15 inch baking sheet with rim and line it with parchment paper.

2. **Prepare the Cake Batter:**
- In a medium bowl, whisk together the flour, cocoa powder, baking powder, and salt.
- In a large mixing bowl, beat the eggs and granulated sugar with an electric mixer until thick and pale, about 5 minutes.
- Add the sourdough discard and vanilla extract, and mix until combined.
- Gently fold in the dry ingredients until just combined.

3. **Bake the Cake:**
- Pour the batter into the prepared baking sheet and spread it evenly with an offset spatula.
- Bake in the preheated oven for 12-15 minutes, or until the cake springs back when lightly touched.

4. **Roll the Cake:**
- Dust a clean kitchen towel with powdered sugar.
- Immediately after removing the cake from the oven, invert it onto the prepared towel.
- Carefully peel off the parchment paper and roll the cake up in the towel, starting from the short end. Let it cool completely.

5. **Prepare the Filling:**
- In a large mixing bowl, beat the heavy whipping cream, powdered sugar, and vanilla extract until stiff peaks form.

6. **Unroll and Fill the Cake:**
- Once the cake is completely cool, unroll it gently.
- Spread the whipped cream filling evenly over the cake.
- Re-roll the cake (without the towel) and place it seam side down on a serving platter.

7. **Prepare the Frosting:**
- In a large mixing bowl, beat the softened butter until creamy.
- Gradually add the powdered sugar and cocoa powder, beating well after each addition.
- Add the vanilla extract and 2 tablespoons of milk. Beat until smooth and creamy, adding more milk if necessary to reach a spreadable consistency.

8. **Frost the Cake:**
- Spread the frosting over the outside of the rolled cake with an offset spatula, creating a bark-like texture to resemble a log.

9. **Decorate:**
- Dust with powdered sugar to resemble snow, and decorate with meringue mushrooms, holly leaves, or other festive decorations if desired.

10. **Serving:**
- Slice and serve the yule log at room temperature.

11. **Storage:**
- Store any leftover yule log in an airtight container in the refrigerator for up to 3 days. Bring to room temperature before serving.

STOLLEN

Calories 210; Fat 8 g; Carb 30 g; Protein 4 g

SERVINGS: 10-12

PREP TIME: 30 minutes | RISING TIME: 4-6 hours | BAKING TIME: 40-50 minutes

UTENSILS:

- Large mixing bowl
- Measuring cups and spoons
- Kitchen scale
- Whisk
- Baking sheet
- Parchment paper
- Pastry brush
- Clean kitchen towel

INGREDIENTS:

- 1 cup (8 oz) sourdough discard
- 3 cups (13.5 oz) all-purpose flour
- 1/2 cup (4 oz) granulated sugar
- 1/2 cup (4 oz) warm milk (dairy or non-dairy)
- 1/2 cup (4 oz) unsalted butter, melted (or dairy-free substitute)
- 1/2 cup (4 oz) dried fruit (such as raisins, currants, or chopped dried apricots)
- 1/4 cup (2 oz) chopped nuts (such as almonds or walnuts)
- 1/4 cup (2 oz) candied citrus peel
- 2 large eggs
- 2 teaspoons vanilla extract
- 1 teaspoon ground cinnamon
- 1/2 teaspoon ground nutmeg
- 1/4 teaspoon ground cardamom (optional)
- 1/4 teaspoon ground cloves (optional)
- 1/2 teaspoon salt
- 2 teaspoons instant yeast (optional, for a quicker rise)

For the Filling:
- 1/2 cup (4 oz) marzipan or almond paste

For the Topping:
- 1/4 cup (2 oz) melted butter
- 1/2 cup (4 oz) powdered sugar

INSTRUCTIONS:

1. **Prepare the Dough:**
- In a large mixing bowl, whisk together the sourdough discard, warm milk, melted butter, granulated sugar, eggs, and vanilla extract until well combined.
- In a separate bowl, mix the flour, cinnamon, nutmeg, cardamom (if using), cloves (if using), salt, and instant yeast (if using).
- Gradually add the dry ingredients to the wet ingredients, mixing until a soft dough forms.
- Knead the dough on a lightly floured surface for about 5-7 minutes until smooth and elastic.

2. **First Rise:**
- Place the dough back into the mixing bowl, cover with a clean kitchen towel, and let it rise at room temperature for 4-6 hours, or until it has doubled in size.
- Prepare the Add-ins:
- While the dough is rising, prepare the dried fruit, chopped nuts, and candied citrus peel.

3. **Incorporate the Add-ins:**
- Once the dough has risen, turn it out onto a lightly floured surface. Gently knead in the dried fruit, chopped nuts, and candied citrus peel until evenly distributed.

4. **Shape the Stollen:**
- Roll the dough out into a rectangle approximately 1/2 inch thick. Place the marzipan or almond paste in a log shape along the center of the rectangle.
- Fold the dough over the marzipan, sealing the edges to encase the filling. Shape the dough into a loaf, tapering the ends slightly.

5. **Second Rise:**
- Place the shaped dough onto a parchment-lined baking sheet. Cover with a clean kitchen towel and let it rise for another 1-2 hours, or until it has puffed up.

6. **Preheat the Oven:**
- About 30 minutes before baking, preheat your oven to 350°F (175°C).

7. **Bake the Stollen:**
- Bake in the preheated oven for 40-50 minutes, or until the stollen is golden brown and sounds hollow when tapped on the bottom. If the top browns too quickly, cover it loosely with aluminum foil.

8. **Apply the Topping:**
- Remove the stollen from the oven and immediately brush it with melted butter.
- Generously dust the stollen with powdered sugar while it is still warm.

9. **Cooling:**
- Let the stollen cool completely on a wire rack.

10. **Serving:**
- Slice and serve the stollen at room temperature. It pairs well with coffee or tea.

11. **Storage:**
- Store any leftover stollen in an airtight container at room temperature for up to 1 week. For longer storage, wrap the stollen tightly in plastic wrap and then in aluminum foil before freezing for up to 3 months. Bring to room temperature before serving.

HOT CROSS BUNS

Calories 170; Fat 5 g; Carb 28 g; Protein 4 g

SERVINGS:
8-10

PREP TIME: 30 minutes   **RISING TIME:** 4-6 hours   **COOLING TIME:** 20-25 minutes

---

UTENSILS:

- Large mixing bowl
- Measuring cups and spoons
- Kitchen scale
- Whisk
- Baking sheet
- Parchment paper
- Pastry brush
- Clean kitchen towel
- Piping bag or ziplock bag

INGREDIENTS:

For the Dough:
- 1 cup (8 oz) sourdough discard
- 3 cups (13.5 oz) all-purpose flour
- 1/2 cup (4 oz) warm milk (dairy or non-dairy)
- 1/4 cup (2 oz) granulated sugar
- 1/4 cup (2 oz) unsalted butter, melted (or dairy-free substitute)
- 2 large eggs
- 1 teaspoon vanilla extract
- 1 teaspoon ground cinnamon
- 1/2 teaspoon ground nutmeg
- 1/4 teaspoon ground cloves (optional)
- 1/2 teaspoon salt
- 1/2 cup (4 oz) dried fruit (such as currants, raisins, or mixed peel)
- 2 teaspoons instant yeast (optional, for a quicker rise)

For the Crosses:
- 1/2 cup (2 oz) all-purpose flour
- 1/4 cup (2 oz) water

For the Glaze:
- 1/4 cup (2 oz) apricot jam or honey

INSTRUCTIONS:

1. **Prepare the Dough:**
- In a large mixing bowl, whisk together the sourdough discard, warm milk, melted butter, granulated sugar, eggs, and vanilla extract until well combined.
- In a separate bowl, mix the flour, cinnamon, nutmeg, cloves (if using), salt, and instant yeast (if using).
- Gradually add the dry ingredients to the wet ingredients, mixing until a soft dough forms.
- Knead the dough on a lightly floured surface for about 5-7 minutes until smooth and elastic.

2. **First Rise:**
- Place the dough back into the mixing bowl, cover with a clean kitchen towel, and let it rise at room temperature for 4-6 hours, or until it has doubled in size.

3. **Prepare the Add-ins:**
- While the dough is rising, prepare the dried fruit.

4. **Incorporate the Add-ins:**
- Once the dough has risen, turn it out onto a lightly floured surface. Gently knead in the dried fruit until evenly distributed.

5. **Shape the Buns:**
- Divide the dough into 12 equal pieces.
- Roll each piece into a ball and place them on a parchment-lined baking sheet, spaced about 1 inch apart.

6. **Second Rise:**
- Cover the buns with a clean kitchen towel and let them rise for another 1-2 hours, or until they have puffed up and hold an indentation when gently pressed.

7. **Preheat the Oven:**
- About 30 minutes before baking, preheat your oven to 375°F (190°C).

8. **Prepare the Crosses:**
- In a small bowl, mix the flour and water to form a thick paste.
- Transfer the paste to a piping bag or ziplock bag with the corner snipped off.
- Pipe a cross onto the top of each bun.

9. **Bake the Buns:**
- Bake in the preheated oven for 20-25 minutes, or until the buns are golden brown and sound hollow when tapped on the bottom.

10. **Apply the Glaze:**
- While the buns are still warm, gently heat the apricot jam or honey until it becomes liquid.
- Brush the warm glaze over the tops of the buns to give them a shiny finish.

11. **Cooling:**
- Let the buns cool completely on a wire rack.

12. **Serving:**
- Serve the hot cross buns at room temperature. They pair well with butter and a cup of tea.

13. **Storage:**
- Store any leftover buns in an airtight container at room temperature for up to 3 days. For longer storage, freeze the buns for up to 3 months. Reheat in the oven or microwave before serving.

EASTER BREAD

Calories 180; Fat 6 g; Carb 28 g; Protein 4 g

**SERVINGS:
8-10**

PREP TIME: 30 minutes	RISING TIME: 4-6 hours	BAKING TIME: 25-30 minutes

UTENSILS:

- Large mixing bowl
- Measuring cups and spoons
- Kitchen scale
- Whisk
- Baking sheet or round cake pan
- Parchment paper
- Pastry brush
- Clean kitchen towel

INGREDIENTS:

- 1 cup (8 oz) sourdough discard
- 3 cups (13.5 oz) all-purpose flour
- 1/2 cup (4 oz) granulated sugar
- 1/2 cup (4 oz) warm milk (dairy or non-dairy)
- 1/4 cup (2 oz) unsalted butter, melted (or dairy-free substitute)
- 2 large eggs
- 1 teaspoon vanilla extract
- 1 teaspoon ground cinnamon
- 1/2 teaspoon ground nutmeg
- 1/2 teaspoon salt
- 1/2 cup (4 oz) dried fruit (such as raisins, currants, or mixed peel)
- 1/4 cup (2 oz) chopped nuts (optional)
- 1 teaspoon orange or lemon zest (optional)
- 2 teaspoons instant yeast (optional, for a quicker rise)
- 1 egg, beaten (for egg wash)
- Colored raw eggs (optional, for decoration)

For the Glaze:
- 1 cup (4 oz) powdered sugar
- 1-2 tablespoons milk (dairy or non-dairy)
- 1/2 teaspoon vanilla extract
- Sprinkles (optional)

INSTRUCTIONS:

1. **Prepare the Dough:**
- In a large mixing bowl, whisk together the sourdough discard, warm milk, melted butter, granulated sugar, eggs, and vanilla extract until well combined.
- In a separate bowl, mix the flour, cinnamon, nutmeg, salt, and instant yeast (if using).
- Gradually add the dry ingredients to the wet ingredients, mixing until a soft dough forms.
- Knead the dough on a lightly floured surface for about 5-7 minutes until smooth and elastic.

2. **First Rise:**
- Place the dough back into the mixing bowl, cover with a clean kitchen towel, and let it rise at room temperature for 4-6 hours, or until it has doubled in size.

3. **Prepare the Add-ins:**
- While the dough is rising, prepare the dried fruit, chopped nuts, and zest (if using).

4. **Incorporate the Add-ins:**
- Once the dough has risen, turn it out onto a lightly floured surface. Gently knead in the dried fruit, chopped nuts, and zest until evenly distributed.

5. **Shape the Bread:**
- Divide the dough into three equal pieces. Roll each piece into a long rope about 18 inches in length.
- Braid the three ropes together, starting from the middle and working your way to the ends. Form the braid into a circle or oval and pinch the ends together to seal.

6. **Second Rise:**
- Place the braided dough onto a parchment-lined baking sheet or into a round cake pan. If using colored raw eggs, gently tuck them into the braid.
- Cover with a clean kitchen towel and let it rise for another 1-2 hours, or until it has puffed up.

7. **Preheat the Oven:**
- About 30 minutes before baking, preheat your oven to 375°F (190°C).

8. **Apply the Egg Wash:**
- Brush the top of the braided dough with the beaten egg to give it a golden color when baked.

9. **Bake the Bread:**
- Bake in the preheated oven for 25-30 minutes, or until the bread is golden brown and sounds hollow when tapped on the bottom. If the top browns too quickly, cover it loosely with aluminum foil.

10. **Prepare the Glaze:**
- In a small bowl, whisk together the powdered sugar, milk, and vanilla extract until smooth. Adjust the consistency by adding more milk or powdered sugar as needed.

11. **Apply the Glaze:**
- Once the bread has cooled slightly, drizzle the glaze over the top. Decorate with sprinkles if desired.

12. **Cooling:**
- Let the glazed bread cool completely on a wire rack.

13. **Serving:**
- Slice and serve the Easter bread at room temperature. It pairs well with butter or jam.

14. **Storage:**
- Store any leftover bread in an airtight container at room temperature for up to 3 days. For longer storage, freeze the bread for up to 3 months. Reheat in the oven or microwave before serving.

HALLOWEEN COOKIES

Calories 120; Fat 6 g; Carb 16 g; Protein 2 g

**SERVINGS:
8-10**

UTENSILS:

- Large mixing bowl
- Measuring cups and spoons
- Kitchen scale
- Whisk
- Rolling pin
- Baking sheet
- Parchment paper or silicone baking mat
- Cookie cutters (Halloween shapes)
- Cooling rack

INGREDIENTS:

- 1 cup (8 oz) sourdough discard
- 2 1/2 cups (11.25 oz) all-purpose flour
- 1/2 cup (4 oz) unsalted butter, softened (or dairy-free substitute)
- 1/2 cup (3.75 oz) granulated sugar
- 1/2 cup (3.75 oz) brown sugar, packed
- 1 large egg
- 1 teaspoon vanilla extract
- 1/2 teaspoon baking powder
- 1/2 teaspoon baking soda
- 1/2 teaspoon salt
- 1 teaspoon ground cinnamon (optional)
- 1/4 teaspoon ground nutmeg (optional)
- Food coloring (optional, for decorating)
- Halloween-themed sprinkles (optional, for decorating)

For the Royal Icing (optional):
- 2 cups (8 oz) powdered sugar
- 1-2 tablespoons milk or water
- 1 teaspoon vanilla extract
- Food coloring (optional)

INSTRUCTIONS:

1. **Prepare the Dough:**
- In a large mixing bowl, cream together the softened butter, granulated sugar, and brown sugar until light and fluffy.
- Add the egg and vanilla extract, and mix until well combined.
- Stir in the sourdough discard until fully incorporated.
2. **Combine the Dry Ingredients:**
- In a separate bowl, whisk together the flour, baking powder, baking soda, salt, cinnamon, and nutmeg.
3. **Mix the Dough:**
- Gradually add the dry ingredients to the wet ingredients, mixing until just combined. Do not overmix.
4. **Chill the Dough:**
- Divide the dough into two equal portions. Flatten each portion into a disc, wrap in plastic wrap, and refrigerate for at least 1 hour.
5. **Preheat the Oven:**
- Preheat your oven to 350°F (175°C). Line a baking sheet with parchment paper or a silicone baking mat.
6. **Roll and Cut the Dough:**
- On a lightly floured surface, roll out one disc of dough to about 1/4 inch thickness.
- Use Halloween-themed cookie cutters to cut out shapes. Transfer the cookies to the prepared baking sheet, spacing them about 2 inches apart.
7. **Bake the Cookies:**
- Bake in the preheated oven for 10-12 minutes, or until the edges are lightly golden.
- Remove from the oven and let the cookies cool on the baking sheet for 5 minutes before transferring them to a cooling rack to cool completely.
8. **Decorate the Cookies:**
- If using, prepare the royal icing by whisking together the powdered sugar, milk or water, and vanilla extract until smooth. Add food coloring if desired.
- Decorate the cooled cookies with royal icing, food coloring, and Halloween-themed sprinkles.
9. **Serving:**
- Serve the cookies once the icing has set. Enjoy your spooky and festive treats!
10. **Storage:**
- Store any leftover cookies in an airtight container at room temperature for up to 1 week.

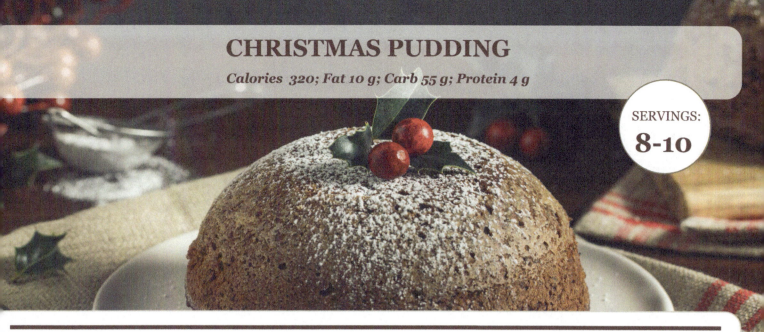

CHRISTMAS PUDDING

Calories 320; Fat 10 g; Carb 55 g; Protein 4 g

SERVINGS:
8-10

PREP TIME: 30 minutes | **COOKING TIME:** 2-3 hours | **AGING TIME:** 2-6 weeks

UTENSILS:

- Large mixing bowl
- Measuring cups and spoons
- Kitchen scale
- Whisk
- Steaming basin or heatproof bowl
- Aluminum foil
- String
- Large pot with lid
- Cooling rack

INGREDIENTS:

- 1 cup (8 oz) sourdough discard
- 1 cup (4 oz) fresh breadcrumbs
- 1 cup (4 oz) all-purpose flour
- 1/2 cup (4 oz) suet or grated cold butter (or dairy-free substitute)
- 1/2 cup (4 oz) brown sugar
- 1/2 cup (4 oz) molasses or dark treacle
- 1/2 cup (4 oz) mixed dried fruit (such as raisins, currants, sultanas, or chopped dates)
- 1/2 cup (4 oz) mixed peel
- 1/4 cup (2 oz) chopped nuts (such as almonds or walnuts)
- 1 medium apple, grated
- 1 medium carrot, grated
- 1/4 cup (2 oz) dark rum, brandy, or orange juice
- 1 teaspoon ground cinnamon
- 1/2 teaspoon ground nutmeg
- 1/2 teaspoon ground allspice
- 1/4 teaspoon ground cloves
- 1/2 teaspoon baking powder
- 2 large eggs
- Zest of 1 lemon
- Zest of 1 orange

For Serving:
- Brandy butter, custard, or cream

INSTRUCTIONS:

1. **Prepare the Fruit Mixture:**
- In a large mixing bowl, combine the mixed dried fruit, mixed peel, chopped nuts, grated apple, grated carrot, and dark rum (or brandy or orange juice). Let this mixture sit for at least 30 minutes to allow the fruit to soak up the liquid.
2. **Prepare the Dry Ingredients:**
- In a separate bowl, whisk together the breadcrumbs, flour, suet (or grated cold butter), brown sugar, ground cinnamon, ground nutmeg, ground allspice, ground cloves, and baking powder.
3. **Combine the Ingredients:**
- Add the dry ingredients to the fruit mixture and stir to combine.
- Add the sourdough discard, molasses, eggs, lemon zest, and orange zest to the mixture. Stir until well combined.
4. **Prepare the Steaming Basin:**
- Grease a steaming basin or heatproof bowl. Spoon the pudding mixture into the basin, pressing down lightly to remove any air pockets.
- Cover the basin with a layer of parchment paper, then a layer of aluminum foil. Tie securely with string, leaving a string handle for easy removal.
5. **Steam the Pudding:**
- Place a trivet or an upturned saucer in the bottom of a large pot. Set the pudding basin on the trivet.
- Fill the pot with water until it reaches halfway up the sides of the basin. Bring to a boil, then reduce to a simmer. Cover the pot with a lid and steam the pudding for 2-3 hours, checking occasionally to ensure the water level remains constant, adding more boiling water if necessary.
6. **Cool the Pudding:**
- Once cooked, carefully remove the pudding basin from the pot. Let it cool completely on a cooling rack.
7. **Aging the Pudding:**
- Once cooled, remove the parchment paper and foil, and replace with fresh parchment paper and foil. Store the pudding in a cool, dark place for 2-6 weeks to allow the flavors to mature.
8. **Reheat the Pudding:**
- To serve, steam the pudding again for about 1 hour to reheat.
9. **Serving:**
- Serve the hot pudding with brandy butter, custard, or cream.
10. **Storage:**
- Store any leftover pudding in an airtight container in the refrigerator for up to 2 weeks. Reheat by steaming before serving.

ANNIVERSARY CAKE

Calories 350; Fat 15 g; Carb 50 g; Protein 4 g

**SERVINGS:
12-16**

PREP TIME: 30 minutes   **BAKING TIME:** 30-35 minutes   **COOLING TIME:** 1 hour

---

UTENSILS:

- Large mixing bowl
- Measuring cups and spoons
- Kitchen scale
- Whisk
- Two 9-inch round cake pans
- Parchment paper
- Cooling rack
- Offset spatula (for frosting)

INGREDIENTS:

For the Cake:
- 1 cup (8 oz) sourdough discard
- 2 1/2 cups (11.25 oz) all-purpose flour
- 1 1/2 cups (12 oz) granulated sugar
- 1/2 cup (4oz) unsalted butter, softened (or dairy-free substitute)
- 1/2 cup (4 oz) vegetable oil
- 1 cup (8 oz) milk (dairy or non-dairy)
- 3 large eggs
- 2 teaspoons vanilla extract
- 2 1/2 teaspoons baking powder
- 1/2 teaspoon baking soda
- 1/2 teaspoon salt

For the Frosting:
- 1 cup (8oz) unsalted butter, softened (or dairy-free substitute)
- 4 cups (16 oz) powdered sugar
- 1/4 cup (2 oz) milk (dairy or non-dairy)
- 2 teaspoons vanilla extract
- Food coloring (optional)
- Fresh berries or edible flowers (optional, for decoration)

INSTRUCTIONS:

1. **Preheat the Oven:**
- Preheat your oven to 350°F (175°C). Grease and line two 9-inch round cake pans with parchment paper.
2. **Prepare the Cake Batter:**
- In a large mixing bowl, cream together the softened butter, vegetable oil, and granulated sugar until light and fluffy.
- Add the eggs one at a time, beating well after each addition. Stir in the vanilla extract and sourdough discard until well combined.
- In a separate bowl, whisk together the flour, baking powder, baking soda, and salt.
- Gradually add the dry ingredients to the wet ingredients, alternating with the milk, beginning and ending with the dry ingredients. Mix until just combined.
3. **Bake the Cakes:**
- Divide the batter evenly between the prepared cake pans and smooth the tops with an offset spatula.
- Bake in the preheated oven for 30-35 minutes, or until a toothpick inserted into the center of the cakes comes out clean.
- Remove the cakes from the oven and let them cool in the pans for 10 minutes. Then, transfer the cakes to a cooling rack to cool completely.
4. **Prepare the Frosting:**
- In a large mixing bowl, beat the softened butter until creamy.
- Gradually add the powdered sugar, 1 cup at a time, beating well after each addition.
- Add the milk and vanilla extract, and beat until the frosting is light and fluffy.
- If desired, divide the frosting into separate bowls and add food coloring to each bowl to create different colors.
5. **Assemble the Cake:**
- Once the cakes are completely cool, place one cake layer on a serving plate or cake stand.
- Spread a layer of frosting over the top of the first cake layer.
- Place the second cake layer on top of the frosting.
- Frost the top and sides of the cake with the remaining frosting, using an offset spatula to create a smooth finish.
6. **Decorate:**
- Decorate the cake with fresh berries or edible flowers if desired.
7. **Serving:**
- Slice and serve the cake at room temperature.
8. **Storage:**
- Store any leftover cake in an airtight container at room temperature for up to 3 days. For longer storage, refrigerate the cake for up to a week or freeze for up to 3 months. Bring to room temperature before serving.

GRADUATION CUPCAKES

Calories 200; Fat 8 g; Carb 30 g; Protein 3 g

SERVINGS:
12-16

PREP TIME: 20 minutes   **BAKING TIME:** 18-20 minutes   **COOKING TIME:** 1 hours

UTENSILS:

- Large mixing bowl
- Measuring cups and spoons
- Kitchen scale
- Whisk
- Muffin tin
- Cupcake liners
- Cooling rack
- Piping bag and tips (for frosting)

INGREDIENTS:

For the Cupcakes:
- 1 cup (8 oz) sourdough discard
- 1 1/2 cups (6.75 oz) all-purpose flour
- 1 cup (8 oz) granulated sugar
- 1/2 cup (4oz) unsalted butter, softened (or dairy-free substitute)
- 1/2 cup (4 oz) milk (dairy or non-dairy)
- 2 large eggs
- 1 teaspoon vanilla extract
- 1 teaspoon baking powder
- 1/2 teaspoon baking soda
- 1/2 teaspoon salt

For the Frosting:
- 1 cup (8 oz) unsalted butter, softened (or dairy-free substitute)
- 4 cups (16 oz) powdered sugar
- 1/4 cup (2 oz) milk (dairy or non-dairy)
- 2 teaspoons vanilla extract
- Food coloring (optional)
- Graduation-themed decorations (e.g., edible toppers, sprinkles, mini diplomas)

INSTRUCTIONS:

1. **Preheat the Oven:**
- Preheat your oven to 350°F (175°C). Line a muffin tin with cupcake liners.
2. **Prepare the Cupcake Batter:**
- In a large mixing bowl, cream together the softened butter and granulated sugar until light and fluffy.
- Add the eggs and vanilla extract, and mix until well combined.
- Stir in the sourdough discard and milk until fully incorporated.
- In a separate bowl, whisk together the flour, baking powder, baking soda, and salt.
- Gradually add the dry ingredients to the wet ingredients, mixing until just combined.
3. **Bake the Cupcakes:**
- Divide the batter evenly among the cupcake liners, filling each about 2/3 full.
- Bake in the preheated oven for 18-20 minutes, or until a toothpick inserted into the center of the cupcakes comes out clean.
- Let the cupcakes cool in the tin for 5 minutes, then transfer to a cooling rack to cool completely.
4. **Prepare the Frosting:**
- In a large mixing bowl, beat the softened butter until creamy.
- Gradually add the powdered sugar, 1 cup at a time, beating well after each addition.
- Add the milk and vanilla extract, and beat until the frosting is light and fluffy.
- If desired, divide the frosting into separate bowls and add food coloring to each bowl to create different colors.
5. **Frost the Cupcakes:**
- Once the cupcakes are completely cool, frost them with the prepared frosting using a piping bag and tips to create decorative swirls or patterns.
6. **Decorate:**
- Decorate the frosted cupcakes with graduation-themed decorations, such as edible toppers, sprinkles, or mini diplomas.
7. **Serving:**
- Arrange the decorated cupcakes on a platter or cupcake stand and serve at room temperature.
8. **Storage:**
- Store any leftover cupcakes in an airtight container at room temperature for up to 3 days. For longer storage, refrigerate the cupcakes for up to a week or freeze for up to 3 months. Bring to room temperature before serving.

ITALIAN WEDDING COOKIES (ANGINETTI)

Calories 120; Fat 5 g; Carb 18 g; Protein 2 g

SERVINGS: 24-30

PREP TIME: 20 minutes   **CHILLING TIME:** 30 minutes   **BAKING TIME:** 15-18 minutes   **COOLING TIME:** 10 minutes

UTENSILS:

- Large mixing bowl
- Measuring cups and spoons
- Kitchen scale
- Whisk
- Baking sheet
- Parchment paper or silicone baking mat
- Cooling rack

INGREDIENTS:

- 1 cup (8 oz) sourdough discard
- 1 cup (8oz) unsalted butter, softened (or dairy-free substitute)
- 1/2 cup (2 oz) powdered sugar
- 2 teaspoons vanilla extract
- 2 cups (9 oz) all-purpose flour
- 1 cup (4 oz) finely chopped nuts (such as pecans, walnuts, or almonds)
- 1/4 teaspoon salt
- Zest of 1 lemon
- 2 large eggs
- 1 teaspoon baking powder
- 1 teaspoon anise extract (optional, for a traditional flavor)
- For the Glaze:
- 2 cups (8 oz) powdered sugar
- 2-3 tablespoons milk or lemon juice
- 1 teaspoon vanilla extract
- Colored sprinkles (optional)

INSTRUCTIONS:

1. **Prepare the Dough:**
- In a large mixing bowl, cream together the softened butter and powdered sugar until light and fluffy.
- Add the vanilla extract, anise extract (if using), lemon zest, and sourdough discard. Mix until well combined.
- In a separate bowl, whisk together the flour, salt, and baking powder.
- Gradually add the dry ingredients to the wet ingredients, mixing until just combined.
- Fold in the finely chopped nuts.
- Add the eggs one at a time, mixing well after each addition until the dough is smooth.
2. **Chill the Dough:**
- Divide the dough into two equal portions. Shape each portion into a disc, wrap in plastic wrap, and refrigerate for at least 30 minutes.
3. **Preheat the Oven:**
- Preheat your oven to 350°F (175°C). Line a baking sheet with parchment paper or a silicone baking mat.
4. **Shape the Cookies:**
- Roll the chilled dough into 1-inch balls and place them on the prepared baking sheet, spacing them about 2 inches apart.
5. **Bake the Cookies:**
- Bake in the preheated oven for 15-18 minutes, or until the cookies are set and the bottoms are lightly golden.
- Remove from the oven and let the cookies cool on the baking sheet for 5 minutes, then transfer to a cooling rack to cool completely.
6. **Prepare the Glaze:**
- Once the cookies are completely cool, roll them in powdered sugar until well coated.
- For an extra festive touch, roll the cookies in powdered sugar a second time before serving.
7. **Decorate:**
- In a medium bowl, whisk together the powdered sugar, milk or lemon juice, and vanilla extract until smooth.
- Dip the top of each cooled cookie into the glaze, allowing any excess to drip off.
- Place the glazed cookies back on the cooling rack and decorate with colored sprinkles, if desired. Allow the glaze to set.
8. **Serving:**
- Arrange decorated cookies on a platter or cupcake stand and serve at room temperature.
9. **Storage:**
- Store any leftover cookies in an airtight container at room temperature for up to 1 week. For longer storage, freeze the cookies for up to 3 months. Bring to room temperature before serving.

SAINT PATRICK'S DAY BREAD

Calories 180; Fat 5 g; Carb 30 g; Protein 3 g

PREP TIME: 20 minutes	BAKING TIME: 30-35 minutes	RISING TIME: 4-6 hours

UTENSILS:

- Large mixing bowl
- Measuring cups and spoons
- Kitchen scale
- Whisk
- Dutch oven or bread loaf pan
- Parchment paper
- Cooling rack

INGREDIENTS:

- 1 cup (8 oz) sourdough discard
- 3 cups (13.5 oz) all-purpose flour
- 1 cup (8 oz) whole wheat flour
- 1 1/2 cups (12 oz) buttermilk (or milk with 1 tablespoon vinegar)
- 1/4 cup (2 oz) honey or molasses
- 1 teaspoon baking soda
- 1 teaspoon salt
- 1 cup (6 oz) raisins or currants
- 1 tablespoon caraway seeds (optional)

INSTRUCTIONS:

1. **Prepare the Dough:**
- In a large mixing bowl, whisk together the sourdough discard, buttermilk, and honey or molasses until well combined.
- In a separate bowl, mix the all-purpose flour, whole wheat flour, baking soda, and salt.
- Gradually add the dry ingredients to the wet ingredients, mixing until a sticky dough forms.
- Fold in the raisins or currants and caraway seeds (if using).
2. **First Rise:**
- Cover the bowl with a clean kitchen towel and let the dough rise at room temperature for 4-6 hours, or until it has doubled in size.
3. **Preheat the Oven:**
- Preheat your oven to 375°F (190°C). If using a Dutch oven, place it in the oven to preheat.
4. **Shape the Dough:**
- Turn the risen dough out onto a lightly floured surface. Shape it into a round loaf or oval, depending on your preference.
- If using a bread loaf pan, line it with parchment paper and place the dough in the pan.
5. **Score the Dough:**
- Use a sharp knife to score an "X" on the top of the dough. This will help the bread expand properly as it bakes.
6. **Bake the Bread:**
- If using a Dutch oven, carefully remove it from the oven and place the dough inside on a piece of parchment paper. Cover with the lid.
- Bake in the preheated oven for 30-35 minutes, or until the bread is golden brown and sounds hollow when tapped on the bottom.
- If using a Dutch oven, remove the lid during the last 10 minutes of baking to allow the top to brown.
7. **Cool the Bread:**
- Remove the bread from the oven and transfer it to a cooling rack. Let it cool completely before slicing.
8. **Serving:**
- Slice and serve the bread with butter, jam, or your favorite spread. It pairs wonderfully with Irish butter and a hot cup of tea.
9. **Storage:**
- Store any leftover bread in an airtight container at room temperature for up to 3 days. For longer storage, freeze the bread for up to 3 months. Reheat in the oven or toaster before serving.

THANKSGIVING STUFFING

Calories 250; Fat 12 g; Carb 28 g; Protein 8 g

SERVINGS:
8-10

PREP TIME: 35 minutes

BAKING TIME: 65-75 minutes

UTENSILS:

- Large mixing bowl
- Measuring cups and spoons
- Loaf pan
- Baking sheet
- Large skillet
- Spatula or wooden spoon
- Knife and cutting board
- Aluminum foil
- Greased baking dish

INGREDIENTS:

For the Sourdough Discard Bread:
- 2 cups sourdough discard
- 1 cup all-purpose flour
- 1/2 cup water
- 1/2 teaspoon salt
- 1/2 teaspoon baking soda

For the Stuffing:
- 1 large loaf of sourdough discard bread (from above or use store-bought)
- 1/2 cup unsalted butter
- 1 large onion, finely chopped
- 2-3 celery stalks, finely chopped
- 2-3 cloves garlic, minced
- 1 teaspoon dried sage
- 1 teaspoon dried thyme
- 1 teaspoon dried rosemary
- 1/2 teaspoon salt
- 1/2 teaspoon black pepper
- 2-3 cups chicken or vegetable broth (adjust based on desired moisture level)
- 2 large eggs, beaten
- 1/4 cup fresh parsley, chopped

INSTRUCTIONS:

1. **Make the Sourdough Discard Bread:**
- Preheat your oven to 375°F (190°C).
- In a large bowl, combine sourdough discard, flour, water, salt, and baking soda. Mix until a dough forms.
- Pour the dough into a greased loaf pan and bake for 25-30 minutes, or until a toothpick inserted into the center comes out clean.
- Allow the bread to cool completely, then cut it into cubes.

2. **Prepare the Stuffing:**
- Preheat your oven to 350°F (175°C).
- Spread the sourdough cubes on a baking sheet and toast in the oven for about 10-15 minutes, or until they are dry and lightly golden. Set aside to cool.
- In a large skillet, melt the butter over medium heat. Add the chopped onion, celery, and garlic. Sauté until the vegetables are tender, about 10 minutes.
- Add the sage, thyme, rosemary, salt, and pepper to the skillet. Stir to combine and cook for another 2 minutes.
- In a large mixing bowl, combine the toasted sourdough cubes with the sautéed vegetables and herbs.
- Pour in the broth gradually, tossing the mixture gently until the bread is evenly moistened but not soggy.
- Stir in the beaten eggs and fresh parsley.

3. **Bake the Stuffing:**
- Transfer the stuffing mixture to a greased baking dish.
- Cover with aluminum foil and bake for 30 minutes.
- Remove the foil and bake for an additional 15-20 minutes, or until the top is crispy and golden brown.
- Let the stuffing cool for a few minutes before serving.

4. **Serving:**
- Serve the stuffing warm as a side dish to your Thanksgiving meal.
- Garnish with additional fresh parsley if desired.
- Pair it with turkey, gravy, and your favorite Thanksgiving sides.

5. **Storage:**
- Store leftover stuffing in an airtight container in the refrigerator for up to 3 days. Reheat in the oven before serving.

SAVORY TARTLETS FOR NEW YEAR

Calories 150; Fat 10 g; Carb 10 g; Protein 3 g

PREP TIME: 30 minutes   **BAKING TIME:** 15-20 minutes

UTENSILS:

- Large mixing bowl
- Measuring cups and spoons
- Kitchen scale
- Whisk
- Muffin tin
- Rolling pin
- Parchment paper or silicone baking mat

INGREDIENTS:

For the Crust:
- 1 cup (8 oz) sourdough discard
- 1 1/2 cups (6.75 oz) all-purpose flour
- 1/2 cup (4 oz) unsalted butter, cold and cubed
- 1/4 teaspoon salt
- 2-3 tablespoons cold water

For the Filling:
- 1/2 cup (4 oz) ricotta cheese
- 1/2 cup (4 oz) grated Parmesan cheese
- 1/4 cup (2 oz) chopped sun-dried tomatoes
- 1/4 cup (2 oz) chopped fresh spinach
- 1 clove garlic, minced
- Salt and pepper to taste
- Fresh basil or parsley for garnish (optional)

INSTRUCTIONS:

1. **Prepare the Crust:**
- In a large mixing bowl, combine the sourdough discard, flour, cold butter, and salt. Mix until the dough resembles coarse crumbs.
- Add cold water, one tablespoon at a time, until the dough comes together. Form the dough into a disc, wrap in plastic wrap, and refrigerate for at least 30 minutes.
2. **Preheat the Oven:**
- Preheat your oven to 375°F (190°C). Grease a muffin tin or line with parchment paper.
3. **Roll Out the Dough:**
- On a lightly floured surface, roll out the chilled dough to about 1/8 inch thickness.
- Use a round cookie cutter or a glass to cut circles from the dough and press them into the muffin tin to form the tartlet shells.
4. **Prepare the Filling:**
- In a medium bowl, combine the ricotta cheese, Parmesan cheese, chopped sun-dried tomatoes, chopped spinach, minced garlic, salt, and pepper. Mix well.
5. **Assemble the Tartlets:**
- Spoon the filling into the tartlet shells, filling each about 3/4 full.
- Bake in the preheated oven for 15-20 minutes, or until the crust is golden brown and the filling is set.
6. **Serving:**
- Garnish with fresh basil or parsley if desired. Serve warm or at room temperature.
7. **Storage:**
- Store leftover tartlets in an airtight container in the refrigerator for up to 3 days. Reheat in the oven before serving.

HEART-SHAPED COOKIES FOR VALENTINE'S DAY

Calories 120; Fat 6 g; Carb 16 g; Protein 2 g

SERVINGS:
24-30

PREP TIME: 20 minutes   **CHILLING TIME:** 1 hour   **BAKING TIME:** 10-12 minutes   **COOLING TIME:** 15 minutes

UTENSILS:

- Large mixing bowl
- Measuring cups and spoons
- Kitchen scale
- Whisk
- Rolling pin
- Baking sheet
- Parchment paper or silicone baking mat
- Heart-shaped cookie cutters

INGREDIENTS:

- 1 cup (8 oz) sourdough discard
- 1 cup (8 oz) unsalted butter, softened (or dairy-free substitute)
- 1 cup (8 oz) granulated sugar
- 1 large egg
- 2 teaspoons vanilla extract
- 3 cups (13.5 oz) all-purpose flour
- 1 teaspoon baking powder
- 1/2 teaspoon salt

INSTRUCTIONS:

1. **Prepare the Dough:**
- In a large mixing bowl, cream together the softened butter and granulated sugar until light and fluffy, about 3-4 minutes.
- Add the egg and vanilla extract, and mix until well combined.
- Stir in the sourdough discard until fully incorporated.
- In a separate bowl, whisk together the flour, baking powder, and salt.
- Gradually add the dry ingredients to the wet ingredients, mixing until just combined. Do not overmix.
2. **Chill the Dough:**
- Divide the dough into two equal portions. Flatten each portion into a disc, wrap in plastic wrap, and refrigerate for at least 1 hour.
3. **Preheat the Oven:**
- Preheat your oven to 350°F (175°C). Line a baking sheet with parchment paper or a silicone baking mat.
4. **Roll and Cut the Dough:**
- On a lightly floured surface, roll out one disc of dough to about 1/4 inch thickness.
- Use heart-shaped cookie cutters to cut out shapes. Transfer the cookies to the prepared baking sheet, spacing them about 2 inches apart.
5. **Bake the Cookies:**
- Bake in the preheated oven for 10-12 minutes, or until the edges are lightly golden.
- Remove from the oven and let the cookies cool on the baking sheet for 5 minutes before transferring them to a cooling rack to cool completely.
6. **Decorate:**
- Decorate the cooled cookies with royal icing, colored frosting, or sprinkles as desired.
7. **Serving:**
- Serve the cookies at room temperature, arranged on a decorative platter. These heart-shaped cookies are perfect for special occasions like Valentine's Day.
8. **Storage:**
- Store cooled, decorated cookies in a hermetically sealed jar at ambient temperature for a maximum of 7 days. To store for an extended period, place in the refrigerator for a maximum duration of 2 weeks or freeze for a maximum of 3 months. Allow frozen cookies to defrost at room temperature before serving.

RED, WHITE AND BLUE SWIRL BROWNIES FOR INDEPENDENCE DAY

Calories 180; Fat 8 g; Carb 25 g; Protein 3 g

SERVINGS:
12

PREP TIME: 20 minutes

BAKING TIME: 25-20 minutes

UTENSILS:

- Large mixing bowl
- Measuring cups and spoons
- Kitchen scale
- Whisk
- 9x9 inch baking pan
- Parchment paper

INGREDIENTS:

- 1 cup (8 oz) sourdough discard
- 1/2 cup (4 oz) unsalted butter, melted
- 1 cup (8 oz) granulated sugar
- 1/2 cup (2 oz) cocoa powder
- 2 large eggs
- 1 teaspoon vanilla extract
- 1/2 teaspoon baking powder
- 1/4 teaspoon salt
- 1/2 cup (2.25 oz) all-purpose flour
- Red and blue food coloring
- 1/4 cup (2 oz) white chocolate chips

INSTRUCTIONS:

1.   **Preheat the Oven:**
- Preheat your oven to 350°F (175°C). Line a 9x9 inch baking pan with parchment paper.
2.   **Prepare the Brownie Batter:**
- In a large mixing bowl, whisk together the melted butter and granulated sugar until well combined.
- Add the eggs and vanilla extract, and whisk until smooth.
- Stir in the sourdough discard until fully incorporated.
- In a separate bowl, whisk together the cocoa powder, baking powder, salt, and flour.
- Gradually add the dry ingredients to the wet ingredients, mixing until just combined.
3.   **Color the Batter:**
- Divide the brownie batter into three equal parts. Leave one part plain, and color the other two parts red and blue using food coloring.
4.   **Assemble the Brownies:**
- Drop spoonfuls of each colored batter into the prepared baking pan, alternating colors.
- Use a toothpick or knife to swirl the batters together for a marbled effect.
- Sprinkle the white chocolate chips over the top.
5.   **Bake the Brownies:**
- Bake in the preheated oven for 25-30 minutes, or until a toothpick inserted into the center comes out with a few moist crumbs.
- Let the brownies cool completely in the pan before slicing.
6.   **Serving:**
- Serve the brownies at room temperature, arranged on a platter. These colorful brownies are perfect for patriotic celebrations like Independence Day.
7.   **Storage:**
- Store cooled, sliced brownies in a hermetically sealed receptacle at ambient temperature for a maximum of 3 days. To store for an extended period, refrigerate for a maximum of 1 week or freeze for a maximum of 3 months. Thaw frozen brownies at room temperature before serving.

WAYS TO PRESERVE SOURDOUGH DISCARD

Sourdough discard is a beneficial byproduct of preparing sourdough bread; it can be preserved and used in different ways. Storing it properly not only saves waste but also has many culinary possibilities. This chapter will help you keep your sourdough discard fresh and teach you how to use it in various tasty recipes.

Refrigerate in an Airtight Container
One of the easiest ways to preserve sourdough discard is by refrigerating it. To keep the discard from drying out and to stop any bad odors from seeping into it from other food items in the refrigerator, use an airtight container. Ideal containers are those made of glass with lids that fit tightly, although food-grade plastic containers can also work well. After refrigerating, you can extend its usability up to one or more weeks. Make sure the container is properly sealed before storing your sourdough discard in the refrigerator to prevent air leaks, which can cause drying out or contamination. If you have large amounts of discard, store it in smaller containers to minimize air exposure each time you open them.

Freeze in Smaller Portions
Freezing leftover sourdough for long periods offers a great storage alternative. Freeze small portions so you can easily thaw the remnants as needed. The sourdough discard should be separated into ice cube trays, silicone molds, or small freezer bags. While frozen, transfer portions into larger freezer bags or containers. Always label each portion with a freezing date. Sourdough discards stay good for up to three months if stored in a freezer. This method also allows for more flexibility when using this discard in a recipe. You thaw out what you need without wasting it. Ensure that this discard is spread evenly among these molds or bags so that defrosting becomes quicker and even across all parts. Freezing in this way also helps maintain the discard's texture and quality when used later.

Label Containers with Dates
Whether you refrigerate or freeze, it is very important to place dates on your containers. This allows for easy management of your sourdough discard inventory by helping you remember to always use the oldest leftovers first. Correctly labeled sourdough discard eliminates any form of confusion or waste. You can use a permanent marker to write directly onto plastic bags or freezer-safe labels for convenience. If there are differences in the amount of discard contained within each, one may note this next to the date. As a result, choosing the right serving size for your recipes will be easy, and no part of your sourdough discard will go to waste.

Use Glass or Food-safe Plastic Containers
It is important to have food-safe and non-reactive containers while storing sourdough discard. Glass jars with tight lids do not absorb any odors or flavors, thus making them a good option. Food-grade plastic containers are equally suitable and may be easier to freeze because they weigh less and have more flexibility. Nevertheless, this should not be done in metal bowls due to possible interaction with acidic remnants from sourdough. Many people prefer durable glass containers because they are odor and stain-resistant. They are also easy to wash and reuse because they do not wear out easily. If you are choosing plastic, choose one that does not contain BPA; it's specifically designed for food storage and will help you keep quality in your sourdough discard.

Stir Occasionally
In cases where the sourdough discard has been stored in the refrigerator for more than a couple of days, occasional stirring would be good. This ensures equal distribution of the liquid (hooch), which naturally separates at the top of the discard. Stirring maintains consistency while preventing any odors from forming. Regular stirring not only maintains the discard's freshness but also its homogeneity, making incorporating it into recipes easier. If there is any significant separation, stir well before use. For optimal flavor and texture throughout your sourdough-based dishes, ensure this practice every time you cook with it.

Feed Weekly if Small Amount

Feeding can be done weekly for those who only have small quantities of sourdough discard to preserve. The procedure involves introducing an equal-ratio mixture of flour and water into the discard, similar to maintaining a starter dough. By doing so, the discard is kept active and remains fresh while preparing foodstuffs. Furthermore, feeding increases the longevity of the sourdough discard, allowing one to keep it for weeks without losing value. Feeding the discard not only maintains its viability but also improves its taste profile, making your baked products richer in flavor. This method works best when you use the sourdough discard more often than once in a while; hence, it leads to a versatile ingredient that can be applied across many other recipes.

Dehydrate for Flakes

To save some leftovers, you may dry the remaining sourdough into flakes. Pour a thin layer of discard on a parchment-lined baking sheet and dry it by air or in a low-temperature oven. When completely dry, break the dehydrated dough to form flakes and keep them in an airtight container. These can be reconstituted with water and used in different recipes where the unique sourdough flavor is desired. The dehydration process allows you to preserve these qualities without refrigeration by turning the sourdough discard into sourdough flakes. Once dried, it can be stored easily and rehydrated whenever necessary. This technique is suitable for people who only bake occasionally but want to retain the typical flavor of their bread.

Add to Pancake or Waffle Batter

If you have some leftover starter, fold it into your pancake or waffle batter. The latter will taste tangy, while the structure will improve because of sourdough discard. To achieve this, replace some liquid with a discard in your recipe to vary its thickness. This method allows you to use up all those leftovers while enhancing your morning meal. Adding sourdough discard to your pancakes or waffles mix transforms an ordinary breakfast into something extraordinary. It's impossible to get such a taste with any other ingredients cooked naturally using fermented dough, thus significantly improving the flavors' complexity. Moreover, the discard's acidity makes pancakes and waffles rise higher than usual, making them extra light during consumption.

Make Sourdough Crackers

Sourdough crackers are an excellent way to consume leftovers. Mix the leftovers with flour, butter, or oil and your preferred seasonings to make a dough. Roll it until it becomes thin, cut it into sections of your choice, and then bake them until hard. These crackers can be eaten alone or with cheese and dips to bring out the sour taste of sourdough. You can personalize your sourdough crackers with different herbs and spices that suit your taste buds. For unique flavors, you might add rosemary, thyme, sesame seeds, or even a pinch of garlic powder. In addition to using up discards, these tasty homemade snacks pair well with a variety of toppings.

Incorporate into a Flatbread Dough

You get outstanding flavor and texture by incorporating some sourdough discard into the flatbread dough. Simply replace some of the flour and liquid in your flatbread recipe with the leftover discard from making bread dough. The natural fermentation in the discard will make the flatbread softer, more pliable, and improve its taste. It's multifunctional since naan bread, pita bread, or other types of flatbreads can be made using it. Flatbreads made from sourdough discards have slightly tangy flavors that perfectly match any topping or dip. Whether Indian curry is served along naan bread or you want Middle Eastern spread inside pita pockets, adding the discard to one's mixture can do wonders. This type of flatbread is easier to digest because there is more fermentation during baking.

Improve Biscuit Texture

Stir in some sourdough starter batter to enhance the biscuits' flavor and texture. This fermenting culture's acidity interacts chemically with baking soda, resulting in lighter biscuits with a slight tanginess. To achieve a more exciting flavor, replace part of the liquid in your biscuit recipe with some sourdough discard.Biscuits made with sourdough discard have a softer and richer taste. The discard adds great complexity to the flavor, helping the dough rise better. These are ideal for breakfast sandwiches or served with gravy, but you may also like them with butter and jam.

Try Sourdough Pretzels
Sourdough pretzels are an awesome way to enjoy the unique flavor of a spent starter. This last addition creates more flavor in the dough, making them chewy snacks. It is important to follow a traditional pretzel recipe but include sourdough discards in the mixture before boiling and baking. Then, eat these as soon as they are out of the oven. The leftover sourdough makes excellent plain pretzels or can be topped with coarse salt, seeds, or a sweet glaze. The tang would then enhance that familiar old-style pretzel taste, making it an exquisite delicacy for parties or individual usage. The fermentation process gives off a chewiness characteristic of genuine pretzels produced through this method.

Flavor Pizza Crust
Boosting your homemade pizza by adding sourdough discard to its crust ensures a rich taste and improved texture. The acidity adds tanginess while improving the dough's structure. Replace a portion of water in your pizza crust recipe with sourdough leftovers to add more dimension to your pie, making it tastier and unforgettable. Sourdough discards can be used to make your homemade pizza more special. It has a fermented flavor that pairs well with different toppings, such as Margherita or some unique combinations. When properly executed, discard contributes to the crust that is crunchy on the outside and doughy on the inside.

Bake Sourdough Bagels
Sourdough discard gives flavorful, chewy bagels. This residual fermentation of the discard results in a flavorful tanginess, which adds to a regular bagel taste. Substitute some of the liquid components in your recipe with discards. Just boil, bake, and top up with your favorite choice. The fermentation of these bagels made from sourdough discards gives them a delightful chewiness and complex flavor. Different kinds of seeds, cheese, or anything can be added as toppings to these bagels for an authentic touch. Not only does using the discard help enhance the taste, but it also improves texture, making every bite pleasurable.

Use in Focaccia Dough
Sourdough discards transform focaccia dough favorably, adding intensity and a stronger bite. To achieve this, replace part of the liquid in the dough with sourdough discard and follow standard dough preparation procedures. Sprinkle the dough with your choice of herbs, coat with olive oil, and bake until a golden-brown color is achieved. Focaccia made with sourdough discard will have a distinct aroma and a richer flavor. Discard helps create soft but airy insides and slightly crispy crusts on top. When made with garlic cloves and generously covered in olive oil and fresh herbs, this focaccia pairs well with appetizers, side dishes, or sandwiches, rather than serving as a pizza base.

TROUBLESHOOTING

COMMON ISSUES AND SOLUTIONS

Fixing Dense Bread: Reasons why bread might be too heavy include under-proofing, incorrect water-to-flour proportions, and overwork. Ensuring your dough rises in a warm, draft-free place until it doubles in size is essential. To avoid overproofing, check the dough regularly. Gradually incorporate small amounts of water for optimal dough consistency until you achieve the desired texture. Refrain from overworking the dough, as doing so will make a bread crumb tight due to excess gluten. Ensure your sourdough starter is bubbly and active before using it in recipes. Moreover, consider the type of flour you are using; for example, bread flour has a higher protein concentration than all-purpose flour, resulting in lighter crumbs.

Achieving the Perfect Crust: For an excellent crust, bake at high temperatures (a minimum of 450°F/230°C) and use steam. Put some water in a pan placed at the bottom of your oven to make steam. Use a heated baking stone or steel to bake for extra crispiness. Slash the dough before baking so you can control expansion and get an attractive finish. Brush some egg wash or water on top of the loaf to give it a golden, glossy crust. Bake halfway through, turn it around; this gives even browning. The type of oven also affects how well your crust turns out. Convection ovens circulate air better, resulting in more uniform bakes. If your oven does not have this feature, consider investing in a convection fan or manually rotating the bread often.

Understanding Dough Consistency: A pleasing outcome depends on proper dough consistency. A well-hydrated dough should not be sticky but instead smooth and elastic. If it is too sticky, add flour. If dry, add water. After that, knead until a windowpane is formed, indicating the perfect development of gluten. Keep detailed notes on the various flours and hydration levels used to understand how they affect dough consistency. Different brands of flour have different absorption rates, which affect dough consistency. These records will enable one to, over time, regulate their dough.

Preventing Overproofing: Overproofing can cause bread to become crumbly. Watch the dough carefully and adjust the proofing times according to its temperature and behavior. Proofing is slowed down in cooler environments, while warmer surroundings speed it up. To ascertain that bread is not over-proofed, conduct a finger-poke test: subtly press your finger into the dough. When it springs back slowly and leaves a slight indentation, it's ready to be baked.

STORAGE AND PRESERVATION

Storing Baked Goods: Proper storage keeps them fresh. Preserve these goods after they have cooled down by putting them into airtight containers. Another way is to cover them with clean kitchen towels and keep the moisture inside. Most dishes can be put in the refrigerator and stored for up to 3-7 days. To keep baked goods longer, freeze them in freezer-safe bags or containers, indicating the date of preparation on each bag for further recognition of their freshness. For example, parchment paper can be used to separate layers of cake and pastries so they do not stick together. If you store different kinds of baked food, make sure they are completely cooled to prevent sogginess from moisture transfer.

Freezing Baked Goods: After baking, cool the goods completely before tightly wrapping them in plastic wrap or aluminum foil and placing them into freezer-safe bags. For best results, flash freeze rolls and muffins by placing them on a baking sheet until they are solid, then transfer them to a bag. This prevents them from sticking together, allowing you to easily remove individual servings later. Label each bag with the type of bakery product and the date it was frozen to keep track of how long it has been stored. Thaw frozen baked goods at room temperature or reheat them in the oven before consuming. To maintain optimal quality, consume all frozen items within three months.

Keeping Baked Goods Fresh: Put whole-grain baked items that are still fresh into sealed containers along with an apple slice or bread. Foods that won't be eaten within a few days should be frozen immediately. Wrapping stale bread in damp cloth and heating it will help revive its freshness. People often use bread boxes that control humidity and airflow, helping the bread stay fresher for longer. During instances where your cakes dry up too fast, acquire vacuum-sealed containers since they eliminate air, leading to the preservation of freshness beyond expectations.

RECIPE ADJUSTMENTS AND CONVERSIONS

Adjusting Recipes for Altitude: High altitude requires that baking powder or yeast be decreased by about 25%. A bit more liquid and flour are needed to make the dough just right. Bake at a higher temperature and lessen the rising time to avoid over-rising and subsequent collapse. The problem with rise time at high altitudes is that it often happens too quickly, causing air to escape and baked goods like bread and cakes to collapse. Watch the dough carefully while proofing it, as you may need to adjust some things here and there. Additionally, reduce the amount of sugar because its fermentation rate increases with faster yeast activity at high elevations.

Converting Recipes to Gluten-Free: Consider using gluten-free flours such as almond meal, coconut flour, or arrowroot starch, among others. Ingredients like xanthan gum and psyllium husk can also help improve texture in gluten-free products. Additionally, be aware that gluten-free dough often requires extra hydration, as it tends to dry out during baking. Measure exactly when making gluten-free baked goods; they often benefit from resting to allow the flours to fully absorb moisture, resulting in a product with excellent crumb structure after baking. Start experimenting with various combinations of alternative gluten-free flours until you reach your desired taste and texture change. Note that gluten-free dough often feels different in touch than other kinds, thus requiring different ways of handling.

Substituting Ingredients in Sourdough Recipes: Adjust ingredients to meet specific dietary needs or preferences, ensuring the recipe remains versatile and adaptable for different tastes and situations. When substituting ingredients in recipes, it's important to understand the role of each component. For instance, milk alternatives such as almond milk or oat milk can replace cow's milk, while honey can be used instead of sugar for a different sweetness profile. Olive oil is an effective substitute for butter in baking whole wheat bread. Flax or chia seeds combined with water can serve as a substitute for eggs in recipes. However, keep in mind that any ingredient swap can lead to flavor changes and affect the recipe's consistency, even if the proteins remain unchanged. For example, butter can alter the fluidity of your batter, and fats like butter and oil not only add moisture but also enhance the tenderness of bread crumbs. Therefore, if a substitution affects the consistency of your mixture, you may need to adjust the amount of liquid or flour accordingly.

Adapting Recipes for Sourdough Discard: Use extra sourdough starter to avoid waste when making other meals. Ensure your starter continues to be active by feeding it every 12–24 hours while keeping it at room temperature. Freeze the starter if you're not using it for extended periods, and remember to feed it weekly while it's thawed. Keep in mind that discard has a sour taste and alters the texture of the final product. It also replenishes some enzymes critical for yeast fermentation, which can be beneficial during the baking process for products such as cookies, buns, and muffins.

BAKING TECHNIQUES AND TIPS

Tips for Using Whole Grain Flours: Use a little more water when baking with whole wheat flour and allow it to ferment longer. Modify your recipes accordingly, and sometimes add vital wheat gluten for better structure. Whole grains provide taste and nutrition but can also have a denser dough. To lighten the texture, sift the flour to remove large bran pieces or blend it with all-purpose flour. Be patient during the longer fermentation times; this will help the flavors develop fully.

Tips for Measuring Ingredients Accurately: Use a digital weighing scale for accurate measurements. For consistent results, spoon your flour into cups, then level them with a knife. Always view your measuring cups at eye level to ensure accuracy. Precision in portioning is imperative to ensure uniformity in baking practices. If you are using sticky ingredients like molasses or honey, lightly oil the cup or spoon to help them slide out easily when measured. When following a recipe, always consider whether ingredients should be weighed or measured by volume.

Incorporating Spices and Herbs: Spice up your dish with herbs and spices. Fresh or dried herbs, finely chopped, may be used in combinations to create different tastes. Start low and adjust to taste, as seasonings can become overpowering very quickly. Consider how different herbs and spices can complement or contrast, depending on what you want your food to taste like. Savory breads go well with rosemary and thyme, whereas cinnamon and nutmeg serve sweet bakes excellently.

Creating Savory vs. Sweet Bakes: Proportions of ingredients when making savory versus sweet baked goods differ based on the intended taste. For savory bakes, mix some cheese, olives, or sun-dried tomatoes into your dough. On the other hand, for sweet bakes, incorporate dried fruits, nuts, and chocolate chips. Ensure you adjust the sugar and salt quantity accordingly. Use a variety of cheese, spices, and herbs to make your savory dishes unique. When preparing sweet treats, for instance, you may use different kinds of fruits or nuts and flavors like vanilla or almond extracts. One must balance these flavors to achieve more complex baked goods. Always remember that, whether for savory or sweet baking purposes, success is determined by trying out new ingredients while adjusting them to fit one's preference.

Timing Your Bakes Perfectly: Control dough fermentation and proofing using visual cues like the poke test. When it comes to bread, the crust should develop a golden-brown color, and the bread should produce a resonant sound when tapped on the bottom, indicating it's fully baked. The baking duration may differ based on the accuracy of your oven and the dough's condition. Keep a close eye on your bakes; record when you start them, any adjustments made, and other relevant details to help replicate successful results. Additionally, be aware of hot spots in your kitchen to utilize them effectively.

Understanding Fermentation Times: Temperature and the types of ingredients used both affect the fermentation process. Modify the fermentation period according to current conditions for perfect taste and texture. For instance, one should find warm places in cold seasons so that dough can ferment adequately; however, in hot climates, shorten fermenting time. Since sourdough has distinct flavors due to its unique fermentation process, it's crucial to record fermentation times and temperatures in a baking diary. This practice helps ensure consistency and reliability in your baking outcomes, enabling you to replicate successful results.

Making Baked Goods More Nutritious: Boost nutritional value by including whole grains, nuts, seeds, and dried fruits. Replace refined sugar with more natural sweeteners like honey or maple syrup to improve flavor, and stick with a healthier choice. Consider using different types of flour, such as chickpea, almond, or coconut flour, for added nutrients. You can also incorporate fiber-rich ingredients like flaxseeds, chia seeds, and hemp hearts to make your recipes healthier. Additionally, pureeing vegetables such as pumpkin, sweet potato, or carrot can enhance nutrition while adding moisture and taste.

Sourdough Discard Hydration Levels: The moisture content of your sourdough discard affects the results. Adjust for the consistency of different baking goods to keep hydration in check. Higher hydration levels make the dough wetter, while low levels dry it. Understanding and maintaining the right texture requires knowing about hydration levels. If your dough feels overly sticky or less sticky, adjust the amount of liquid or flour used until you get a manageable consistency. Keep track of these percentages for future reference.

Sourdough Discard Flavor Profiles: Sourdough discard creates a tartness that becomes more prominent over longer fermentations. Young discards have a milder taste than old ones with strong sour flavors. Mixing discards from different stages of fermentation gives the bread distinct tastes. Other flavors that can be added to recipes will balance out the acidulated tastes resulting from this process; sugars in dried fruit, among others, can counteract acidity through sweetness and thereby work with it instead of against it. Deliberately making combinations with varying flavors is the best way to do it.

Working with Cold Fermentation: Cold storage allows the dough to rise at a controlled pace, enhancing its flavor and texture. For the final proofing, chill the dough in the refrigerator for 12-24 hours or overnight to develop a better crust and crumb structure. This method also makes the dough easier to handle. Before baking, ensure the dough returns to room temperature for even baking. The lower temperatures during cold fermentation contribute to a deeper flavor and a more open crumb structure. Additionally, this technique offers flexibility, allowing you to prepare and bake your loaves at your convenience.

Best Practices for Sourdough Discard: Use active discards from your bubbling starter. Mix water with discard to create a gentle and natural abrasive cleaner for scrubbing cooking pots and pans. Its tartness helps break down dirt. Always have a regular feeding schedule for your starter, and keep it at an ambient temperature. If you have more discard than you can use, consider sharing it with friends or fellow bakers who might appreciate the tangy addition to their recipes.

Please do not throw away discard, but incorporate it into other foods as much as possible or find ways to use discard differently in cooking or baking recipes. A healthy, active starter ensures that your baking projects come out successful.

Achieving Uniform Bakes: To ensure even baking, distribute dough uniformly and maintain consistent oven temperatures by swapping trays halfway through the baking process. Using an oven thermometer helps achieve precise temperature control, which is crucial for successful baking. Monitor your bakes closely and make adjustments as needed, such as moving baking sheets or using a baking stone to stabilize heat and address uneven browning. Understanding how your oven performs and making these modifications will help you achieve consistent results.

USING DISCARD IN NON-BAKING RECIPES

The bubbly remnant left after feeding your starter goes beyond making sourdough bread. This delicious discard gives a tangy taste to many other dishes besides baked goods. Below are some ideas:

Soups and Stews: Add a spoonful of discard to your soup or stew for increased depth of flavor.
Salad Dressings and Sauces: Whip discard into salad dressings or sauces for improved tanginess and complexity.
Marinades: The acidity in discard makes it a great addition to marinades for meats, enhancing flavor and tenderness.

BATCH BAKING TIPS

Here are some tips to maximize efficiency and get great results.

Double (or Triple) the Recipe: Most recipes scale easily. Doubling or tripling a recipe allows you to bake more than one batch at once so you can freeze some for later.
Plan Your Baking Order: Consider the oven temperature required for each recipe. Bake items requiring similar temperatures consecutively instead of multiple preheats.
Utilize Cooling Racks: Use several cooling racks to maximize counter space. Let baked goods cool completely before storing or freezing.
Organize Your Workspace: Arrange your ingredients and tools efficiently before beginning. This will help to ease the baking process and make it more efficient by reducing the likelihood of missing an ingredient or a step.
Prep Ahead: Pre-measure and prepare ingredients in advance, especially for recipes with multiple components. This can save time during actual baking and ensure that things go much smoother.

SEASONAL BAKING TIPS

Here are suggestions on how to incorporate seasonal flavors:

Summer: Use fresh summer fruits such as berries, peaches, and plums in pies, cobblers, or muffins.
Fall: Spiced cakes, pumpkin bread, cookies with cinnamon, nutmeg, and ginger – warm flavors perfect for the fall season.
Winter: Cozy up with gingerbread cookies, indulgent chocolate desserts, or citrus cakes that brighten even the gloomiest wintry days.
Spring: Celebrate spring with lighter desserts featuring floral flavors like lavender or lemon, or fresh ingredients such as rhubarb and asparagus.

Understanding Oven Temperatures: Baking results are different at various oven temperatures. Use an oven thermometer to make sure it's accurate. Preheat for at least 20 minutes before baking. Experience + recipe requirements = adapted baking times. Recalibrate your oven periodically to maintain accuracy. If your oven is hotter or cooler than most, adjust the temperature settings or use baking stones to even out heat levels. Understanding these quirks can help you achieve better baking results.

UTENSILS AND MAINTENANCE

Cleaning and Maintaining Baking Utensils: Clean mixing bowls, utensils, and baking sheets immediately after use. Check the state of your oven and mixer regularly, and store tools in a dry, contamination-free place. Regular maintenance ensures sharp-cutting implements and prolongs the life of your equipment. Proper care and storage of your baking tools contribute to better results and a more enjoyable baking experience. Invest in high-quality utensils and keep them in good condition to ensure consistent performance.

CONCLUSION

In "The Ultimate Sourdough Discard Cookbook," Esme Whitmore has masterfully showcased sourdough discard's incredible versatility and potential. This cookbook is not just a collection of recipes; it is a comprehensive guide to transforming what is often seen as waste into a wide array of delicious, nutritious, and environmentally friendly dishes.

With detailed instructions, stunning photography, and a focus on sustainability, Esme has created a resource that will inspire and empower you to explore new culinary horizons. Whether you're preparing a simple breakfast, a hearty dinner, or a festive treat, you'll find recipes that cater to all occasions and dietary preferences.

By embracing the sourdough revolution, you'll enhance your cooking and baking skills and contribute to a more sustainable and eco-friendly lifestyle. Esme's dedication to reducing waste and promoting health through fermented foods is a testament to her passion and expertise.

Thank you for joining Esme Whitmore on this culinary journey. May "The Ultimate Sourdough Discard Cookbook" become a cherished companion in your kitchen, guiding you to create meals that are as kind to the planet as they are delightful to the palate. Enjoy the process, savor the flavors, and happy baking!

Made in the USA
Monee, IL
20 December 2024

75003854R00072